THE
LITTLE
BOOK
OF
STAFFORDSHIRE

KATE GOMEZ

First published 2017

The History Press
The Mill, Brimscombe Port
Stroud, Gloucestershire, GL5 2QG
www.thehistorypress.co.uk

British Library Cataloguing in Publication Data.
A catalogue record for this book is available from the British Library.

ISBN 978 0 7509 6482 1

Typesetting and origination by The History Press
Printed and bound in Great Britain by TJ International Ltd

MIX
Paper from
responsible sources
FSC® C013056

CONTENTS

INTRODUCTION AND ACKNOWLEDGEMENTS

Compiling this book has been an adventure, sometimes undertaken alone, but more often with friends and family and special mention must go to Jacky Billingsley, Patti Wills, Joss Musgrove Knibb, Eddie Strain and Maxine Rodger (aka my mum!) for providing knowledge, encouragement and laughs along the way. The stories, information and snippets of trivia contained in this book have been collected from a wide range of sources, and have been a constant reminder that truth is often far stranger, far more interesting and far more entertaining than anything fiction can offer. I thank another friend of mine, who goes by the name of Brownhills Bob, for keeping my excursions into the wilder realms of folklore in check and my spirits up when necessary.

Thanks also to my family for indulging, if not quite understanding, my enthusiasm for local history and to my publishers The History Press for their support and patience.

This book is by no means a comprehensive collection of everything the county has to offer and there are plenty more discoveries to be made. Staffordshire has been my home for twelve years now and this book is dedicated to all the women and men of my adopted county who have made it such an interesting and inspiring place to live, and to all those who continue to do so.

Kate Gomez,
Lichfield, 2017

1

BEFORE STAFFORDSHIRE

The year 2016 marked the 1,000th anniversary of the first mention of Staffordshire in the Anglo Saxon Chronicle and the county celebrated with the inaugural Staffordshire Day. Of course, people lived, worked and died here long before that name existed and evidence of their existence can be found in the landscape that surrounds us.

NEOLITHIC AND BRONZE AGE

The Bridestones sit on the Staffordshire and Cheshire border and are thought to be somewhere between 4,000 and 6,000 years old. It is an absolute wonder that these stones are still standing, and all the more remarkable when you read of their treatment in the past. Back in the eighteenth century, the site was regarded as a convenient quarry and was plundered for its stone, some of which was used to build local houses and some of which was taken to build the nearby turnpike road. There are also rumours that some of the stone can be found in the ornamental gardens at Tunstall Park, which was opened to the public in June 1908. The stones are said to have sustained yet more damage in the nineteenth century, both accidentally, when a fire lit at the site caused the stones to crack, and deliberately, when an engineer working on the Manchester Ship Canal supposedly demonstrated how detonation worked on one of the larger stones. There are stories that claim the stones mark the resting place of a murdered pair of newlyweds, a Saxon woman and her Viking groom. Others say weddings once took place here.

Near to Oakley Hall, at Mucklestone, there is a Neolithic monument frequently referred to as the 'Devil's Ring and Finger', comprising of two large stones, one round with a 20in-diameter porthole in the middle and the other standing 6ft tall. No longer in their original position, they are thought to have been part of a burial chamber and have also been known as 'The Whirl Stones'.

When Thor's Cave in the Manifold Valley was excavated in the late nineteenth and early twentieth century, an assortment of archaeological finds including tools, pottery, beads and at least seven human burials was discovered, suggesting the cave had been in use from the Palaeolithic period through to the Iron Age and Roman periods.

A small copper alloy anvil, used as a Bronze Age gold-working tool, still with tiny gold flecks on its working faces, was discovered by a metal-detectorist at Knowle Hill in Lichfield along with several other objects from the same period, including an adze and a socketed axe.

At the confluence of the rivers Trent and Tame, a series of Neolithic or Early Bronze Age ritual landscape features have been termed the 'Catholme ceremonial complex'. Amongst them are a Woodhenge monument, a 'sunburst' monument, a possible cursus and a large ring ditch.

In August 2015, a Bronze Age cremation urn was discovered at the Roaches by a man repairing a footpath.

A cemetery containing the cremated remains of twenty-one individuals along with the remains of five cinerary urns were discovered during the excavation of two ring ditches in Barton under Needwood in 1996.

A Bronze Age barrow at Leek, known as Cock Low, was destroyed in 1907 to make way for housing. On the 1838 town plan it is shown as a large mound and standing around 4m high. An urn discovered near the top of the mound contained animal and human bone and a heart-shaped carved stone.

A total of twenty-one burnt mounds have been discovered in the county, the majority in the Cannock Chase area.

When the Wardlow barrow was excavated in 1955 it was found to contain a central cremation deposit accompanied by an incense or pygmy cup, three fragments of a reddish-buff vessel, a barbed and tanged arrowhead, flint knives and other flint implements. The barrow was destroyed by the extension of Wardlow Quarry.

IRON AGE

Staffordshire has a number of hillforts including Bunbury Hill in the grounds of Alton Towers, Berth Hill in the Maer Hills, Bishop's Wood near Eccleshall, Bury Bank at Stone, Berry Ring in Stafford, Kinver Edge and Castle Ring at the highest point on Cannock Chase, 240m above sea level – the latter was excavated by a local historian in the nineteenth century.

Local tribes in the area, which would later become Staffordshire, were known as the Cornovii, Coritani and Brigantes.

Four Iron Age coins were discovered near Gnosall in 2011.

The Glascote gold alloy torc was discovered by a canal worker who was told it was a coffin handle and to keep it as a souvenir. In 1970, it was declared treasure and purchased by the people of Birmingham and it has been suggested that it would have been made for a tribal chief. It is similar to a torc discovered in the Needwood Forest suggesting there may have been a craftsman in the area. The local high school was named after the find, as was a street in the vicinity. Other torcs from the period have been discovered near Draycott and Alrewas where three unfinished examples were discovered in 1996.

ROMAN

Just outside of Lichfield, in the village of Wall, are the remains of the Roman settlement of Letocetum, a Latinised version of an Iron Age place name meaning 'grey wood'. The foundations of the bathhouse and guesthouse (or *mansio*), established here to provide rest and recuperation and a change of horses to those travelling along Watling Street, are still visible.

Many fascinating archaeological finds have been unearthed at the site and are displayed in the small site museum, including a carved stone, discovered built into the foundations of the *mansio*, along with seven others currently in storage at Birmingham Museum and Art Gallery. The carving seems to show two horned heads facing each other, with a circular object, interpreted as a shield, to their right. Heads also appear on some of the other stones found alongside it. One depicts a figure with a club in one hand, and a severed head or skull at its feet. Another features a head in what may be some sort of niche and a fourth has a head with an open mouth, which may suggest it is screaming. Carved onto a fifth stone are two 'warrior' figures with shields, standing side by side. A pattern of sorts around their legs has been interpreted as representing water. A second pair of figures, enclosed in a frame or box of some sort, lie at right angles to these 'warriors'. Two further stones have inscriptions, or at least partial inscriptions – 'CUINTI ... CI' and 'DDBRUTI' – and on the eighth stone is a carving resembling a Christian cross, although it may be a pagan symbol representing the sun. All but one of the stones were built into the foundations of the *mansio* in an inverted position, and there is a theory that they were originally part of a Romano-British shrine dedicated to a native god or gods, demolished sometime around the building of the *mansio*.

The reason for the shrine's demolition at this stage is unclear, but it has been suggested that it may have been replaced by a yet to be discovered temple dedicated to a Roman god built elsewhere on the site. Incorporating the stones upside down suggests that the native gods represented by the carvings were still respected, and perhaps even feared by the builders of the *mansio*. A ninth carved stone, found separately in a hypocaust in the north-east of the mansion appears to depict a phallus, and was inserted after construction to provide additional protection for the building.

The late Professor Mick Aston of *Time Team* had one of his first experiences of archaeology at Letocetum, under the guidance of Jim Gould FSA.

Whilst excavating the Wyrley to Essington canal at Pipehill, at the end of the eighteenth century, a 500-yard section of a Roman military barricade (or palisade) made from trunks of oak trees was discovered. It was thought to have originally stretched from Pipe Hill to the Roman settlement at Letocetum.

A lead ingot dating to AD 76, inscribed with the names of the emperor Vespasian and the maker Deceangli, was discovered on Hints Common.

At Chesterton, there was a first-century Roman fort and settlement excavated in 1969.

In 1960, a man digging in his garden on Lightwood Road in the Longton area of Stoke-on-Trent came across an earthenware pot containing over 2,400 coins and two silver bracelets. The find, now at the Potteries Museum and Art Gallery, is known as the Lightwood Hoard.

A Roman fort was established at Rocester in around AD 69, and earthworks are still visible.

A series of Roman military sites, including two forts, several camps and a small, defended settlement known as Pennocrucium, have been identified in the Stretton Mill and Water Eaton area.

ANGLO-SAXON

At Holy Trinity church in Eccleshall, there are two fragments of a Saxon preaching cross, one featuring two figures separated by a tree and the other, a man and horse. The pair of figures on the former have been interpreted by some as Adam and Eve alongside the Tree of Life and the figure on the latter as a possible early representation of St Chad, who was of course the first Bishop of Lichfield. Although there is little other evidence at present, the presence of the cross and the 'Eccles' element of the place name, suggests that there may have been an early Christian community here.

The Staffordshire Hoard is the largest collection of Anglo-Saxon gold and silver metalwork ever discovered. It was found in a field alongside Watling Street, in the parish of Hammerwich in July 2009 by a metal detectorist and consists almost entirely of items associated with warfare. A further eighty-one artefacts were recovered from the site in November 2012. The hoard has been dated to the seventh or eighth century and the finds are jointly owned by Birmingham and Stoke-on-Trent city councils. It is valued at £3.285 million and a fundraising campaign the save the hoard for the nation raised over £900,000 in public donations. Suggestions for why the hoard came to be buried include an offering to pagan gods or an attempt to conceal the items until the owner was able to return to collect them safely.

The Maer Hills are reputed to be the site of a number of battles and King Oswy of Northumbria, killed in AD 642, is said to be buried at Kings Bank.

An Anglo-Saxon burial ground was discovered in 1850 when a large number of urns containing human bones were found at a depth of *c.* 3ft in a gravel pit near Barton Station, opened by the Midland Railway Company. Some of the urns also contained iron weapons, including two knives.

At a cave to the right-hand side of Beeston Tor, sometimes known as St Bertram's Cave, a hoard of four Anglo-Saxon brooches and twenty-three silver pennies of Edmund of East Anglia dating to around AD 875 were discovered in 1924. It is believed that the hoard is related to the invasion of the Danish Great Army into East Anglia in 869, and the murder of King Edmund in the same year.

A Saxon sword and axe were discovered in the park at Alton Towers in 1834.

A decorated Saxon cross shaft was discovered built into the foundations of the north wall of the nave of Lichfield Cathedral and an Anglo-Saxon building, excavated in the Cross Keys area of the city during work on the car park in 2007–08, was found to incorporate reused Roman masonry from the nearby site of Letocetum.

The Battlestone, a Saxon cross unearthed during the building of the new Ilam village, is believed to have been carved to commemorate a battle with the Danes. There are several other

Saxon crosses in and around the church at Ilam, which also features a walled-up Saxon doorway in the south wall.

Several fragments of crosses exist in and around the church of St Peter in Alstonefield. As several of these are unfinished it has been suggested that there may have been a stone carving workshop near to the site of the church during the Anglo-Saxon period.

Three Anglo-Saxon crosses exist in the graveyard of Checkley parish church. Local tradition says they are monuments erected to the memory of three bishops killed in a battle between the Saxons and the Danes at Deadman's Green.

The will of Wulfric Spot dates to the reign of King Aethelred the Unready and so predates the Domesday Book by around eighty years, making it an important source for the study of Staffordshire prior to the Norman Conquest.

2

STAFFORDSHIRE CASTLES AND HOUSES

FIVE CASTLES OF STAFFORDSHIRE

Stafford Castle started out as a classic motte-and-bailey-style fortress after William the Conqueror gave land to Norman lord Robert de Toeni to build a timber castle to keep the locals under control. Around 1350, Ralph, a founder member of the Order of the Garter, became the 1st Earl of Stafford and ordered a stone castle to be built on the existing motte. Humphrey Stafford was created Duke of Buckingham in 1444 and the castle, along with the rest of Stafford's estate, was seized by the Crown who considered Edward's royal blood to be a threat. It was restored to the family but fell into disrepair, with a later Edward Stafford referring to in 1603 as, 'My rotten castle of Stafford'. During the Civil War, the castle was garrisoned by the Royalists and reinforced with men from Lichfield, Tutbury and Dudley who helped Lady Stafford defend the castle from the Roundheads. However, it was eventually captured by the parliamentarians who had it demolished. In the 1790s, only a low wall was visible above ground. Work began to rebuild in the Gothic revival style in 1813, although a lack of funds meant the work was never completed. By the 1950s the structure was unsafe, with the last of its caretakers, who had run a small tearoom at the castle, having left the previous year. In 1961, Lord Stafford gave it to the local authority who called in the army to make it safe following the death of a young boy at the site. Although the only visible stonework is nineteenth century, recent archaeological work suggests that Stafford is one of the best surviving examples of Norman earthworks in the country.

Tamworth Castle overlooks the River Tame on a site that has been fortified since AD 913 when Aethelflaeda, Lady of the Mercians, built a burh to defend the town from the Vikings. It is likely that the motte-and-bailey castle was built around 1070, but was partly destroyed in 1215 when Robert Marmion, the fourth in the line of Marmions owning the castle, deserted King John. The castle was restored to them following King John's death and the castle was transformed from a fortress to a Tudor home under the Ferrers' family. In 1783 the Great Hall at Tamworth castle was whitewashed and a sixteenth-century mural of Sir Lancelot and Sir Tarquin was destroyed. Shortly afterwards, the banqueting hall was used as a forge in connection with Robert Peel's cotton foundry, the stone floor destroyed and replaced by red bricks. In 1897 the castle was sold to Tamworth Corporation for £3,000 and it opened as a museum two years later. It is one of the best-preserved motte-and-bailey castles in England, with the second largest motte in England after that at Windsor Castle.

Chartley Castle is a ruined motte-and-bailey castle between Stafford and Uttoxeter and was one of twenty-two castles built by the 6th Earl of Chester, Ranulf de Blundeville, whose name means 'he who ransacks cities'. There had previously been a wooden castle on the site, built in 1090 by Henry de Ferrers, a standard bearer of William the Conqueror. When Chartley Hall was completed in 1420 the castle was abandoned.

Tutbury Castle was first recorded in 1071 and was the seat of the de Ferrers family until Henry III gave it to his younger son Edmund, Earl of Lancaster. After withstanding a siege that lasted three weeks during the Civil War, the castle was destroyed following an Act of Parliament in 1647–48. The demolition was incomplete, and the ruins still stand today. The castle is perhaps best known for being the prison of Mary, Queen of Scots on several occasions, as she was moved around the Midlands for eighteen years in a bid to thwart rescue attempts. On Christmas Eve 1585, Mary left Tutbury, a place where she had described herself as being subjected to all the 'winds and injures of heaven'. The castle is still owned by the Duchy of Lancaster but is leased to curator Lesley Smith, an English Reformationist Medical Historian and well known for her interpretations of Mary, Queen of Scots, Elizabeth I and other historical figures.

Alton Castle sits above the Churnet Valley on a site fortified since Saxon times. The current castle was built by John Talbot, 16th Earl of Shrewsbury, who commissioned Augustus Pugin to replace the majority of the twelfth-century ruins with a neo-Gothic castle, replica medieval hospital, guildhall and presbytery. In 1855, an order of nuns known as the Sisters of Mercy used the site, with the presbytery becoming their convent. In 1996, it was converted into a Catholic youth retreat centre owned by the Archdiocese of Birmingham.

Other castles in the county include Caverswall, Eccleshall, Heighley, Newcastle-under-Lyme and Stourton.

STAFFORDSHIRE'S LOST HOUSES

In 1761 a young nobleman called Arthur Chichester, the Earl (later Marquess) of Donegall, acquired **Fisherwick Hall,** a 'very proper brick house' built in the late sixteenth century by the Skeffington family. Within five years, Donegall had decided to transform his Tudor home into a fashionable and elegant mansion and enlisted the services of some of the best-known architects and artists of the day to help him. Lancelot 'Capability' Brown was employed to redesign and remodel the house and surrounding parkland. Some of his additions to the Fisherwick landscape included 10,000 trees (earning his employer a medal from the Society of Arts), a ladies' botanic garden, an orangery and the creation of a lake and a cascade. The mansion itself was built from white stone, with a huge Corinthian portico gracing the entrance. Lavish interiors were created by Joseph Bonomi (who is mentioned in Jane Austen's *Sense and Sensibility*), his friend Jean-Francois Rigaud, the stuccoist Joseph Rose, and Thomas Gainsborough was commissioned to paint the Donegall family portraits.

After just half a century, the Donegall era at Fisherwick drew to a close. The marquess died in 1799, and by 1808 the majority of the estate had been bought by Richard Bagot Howard, owner of Elford Hall. Fisherwick Hall was torn down and sold off to the highest bidder. The columns which had once held the portico over the entrance to the hall eventually found their way to the George Hotel, Walsall, in 1823, bought for next to nothing after being found disused and covered in moss (unfortunately as the George Hotel was demolished in 1934, the columns may lie somewhere in this state once again!). The porch is said to have made its way to Upfields Farm on the Elford Road, wrought-iron gates featuring Donegall's initials ended up at Bolehall in Tamworth, and a staircase and doors were made use of in a house in Beacon Street, Lichfield.

Beaudesert, at the edge of Cannock Chase, was the seat of the Paget family, given to one of Henry VIII's closest advisers William Paget following the Reformation. His descendant, Henry Cecil Paget, known as the Dancing Marquess, inherited the title and family estates in 1898. Described by many as a flamboyant eccentric, he converted the chapel at the family's other home, Plas Newydd, into a 150-seat theatre, inviting local people to watch musical comedies and pantomimes, all starring the extravagantly costumed marquess in the lead role.

Paget also took his theatre troupe on tour. In 1903, they performed *The Marriage of Kitty* and *An Ideal Husband* to huge audiences at St James's Hall in Lichfield. This was one of the few times that this marquess actually stayed at Beaudesert. Despite an enormous annual income that made him one of Queen Victoria's wealthiest subjects, the cost of staging his dazzling theatre shows and a love of expensive clothes, perfumes, jewellery and parties left him heavily in debt. In 1904, the contents of Plas Newydd were put up for auction and a sale of some of the contents of Beaudesert followed in January 1905. Later that year, the Marquess died of pneumonia in Monte Carlo aged only 30. The *Lichfield Mercury* reported his death in March 1905 saying, 'The news of Lord Anglesey's death was received at Bangor with much regret, as Lord Anglesey, despite his peculiarities was much liked there.'

It was said that the Dancing Marquess was known to the tenants of his Staffordshire estate only by repute, and that he had neglected his ancestral home. His cousin and successor Charles Paget was determined to do things differently, and in 1906 began to make alterations to Beaudesert in preparation for him spending more time there. Unfortunately, in 1909, with his mother Lady Alexander Paget already in residence, a huge fire broke out at the hall. Fire brigades from Rugeley, Cannock, Hednesford, Brownhills and Lichfield attended the blaze, which began in the servants quarters and destroyed much of the west wing. Perhaps this was the beginning of the end for Beaudesert.

By the early 1920s, the Paget family decided they were unable to run two estates due to the heavy burden of taxation and decided to take up permanent residence at Plas Newydd. What they did not take with them from Beaudesert to Anglesey was put up for sale, including Chinese wallpaper, Flemish tapestries, a Broadwood grand piano and a billiard table. Then in 1932, the entire Beaudesert estate was put up for auction. Although many of its cottages and lodges were sold, the hall itself was not. In 1935, the *Lichfield Mercury* published a letter written by the marquess in response to people's concerns over the future of Beaudesert. In it he explained that the hall had not received one single bid at the 1932 auction, and that despite being offered to every possible public body, colleges, the British Red Cross

Society and school authorities, it had been found unsuitable by all. He added a postscript asking for any practical suggestions, which might yet save Beaudesert.

The fabric of the hall, along with the fixtures and fittings, were sold off piecemeal. Some of the interior furnishings were taken to Carrick Hill in Adelaide, Australia, and what was left was sold to demolition contractors, but the firm went out of business before they could complete the job of razing Beaudesert to the ground. The remains of Beaudesert, including part of the Great Hall, were given listed status in 1953. During demolition many of the bricks from Beaudesert were taken to re-face St James's Palace, which had suffered from pollution as a result of coal smoke. Much of the estate is now used as a Scout and Guide camp, administered by the Beaudesert Trust.

Elford Hall, in the village of the same name between Lichfield and Tamworth, and its associated estate were gifted to Birmingham City Council in July 1936. Francis Paget, who had served in the trenches of the First World War and had vowed to God to do something to benefit others if he were to make it home safely, made the decision in order 'to promote the healthful recreation of the citizens of Birmingham'. Basque children fleeing from the Spanish Civil War were housed in the mansion in 1938 and during the Second World War the hall was used to store artwork from the Birmingham Museum and Art Gallery. When a gale caused a chimneystack to crash through three storeys of the derelict hall in 1962, the Birmingham Corporation made the decision to demolish the hall. All that remained was the Walled Garden, which lay overgrown and neglected and earmarked for a housing development until 2009 when a group of local people formed an action group to restore the garden, retaining as much of its original character whilst also creating somewhere free and accessible for the public to use and enjoy.

Trentham Hall started life as an Augustinian priory but was acquired by the Leveson family, who later married into the

Gower family. Capability Brown landscaped the garden, and the house was doubled in size by the mid nineteenth century. However, by 1907 it had been abandoned as pollution from the Potteries was flowing down the Trent, which had been diverted to create a lake close to the hall and supply water to the fountains; it was said, 'The pools of the princely grounds of Trentham are literally becoming the cesspool of the Potteries'. In 1979, the estate was sold with the hope of transforming it into a leisure park like nearby Alton Towers but subsidence caused by coal mining in the area made this scheme unworkable. During the Second World War it was used by the Bank of England, and Trentham Ballroom opened on the site in 1931 playing host to bands including The Beatles, Pink Floyd and The Who before closing in 2002.

Pillaton Hall was demolished when Sir Edward, the fourth and last of the Littleton baronets, moved the family seat from Pillaton Hall to Teddesley in 1742. The building of the new hall was funded by the discovery of a hoard of gold and silver coins found in twenty-five purses during the demolition of Pillaton.

Drayton Manor was built by the Peel family in 1835, but the family fortunes were frittered away, particularly by the 4th baronet, a gambler, and reputed to be the man who 'broke the bank' at Monte Carlo. Now all that remains of the house is its clock tower and part of the servants' quarters although there was a rumour that the rest of the house had been bought by an American who had rebuilt it back in his home country. The site was used as a training post during the Second World War, and afterwards was purchased by George and Vera Bryan, who opened an amusement park in 1949. George was the son of William Bryan, an inventor of slot machines. A zoo was added in 1954, when the Bryans teamed up with Molly Badham, who would later own Twycross Zoo. Today, Drayton Manor is the fifth most popular theme park in the country.

Ranton Abbey was accidentally burned down in 1942 when Dutch troops forming the bodyguard for Queen Wilhemina of the Netherlands were stationed there.

Biddulph Old Hall was destroyed by the parliamentarians after the Royalist garrison there surrendered during the Civil War. The famous Roaring Meg cannon was used during the attack. After King Charles II was restored to the throne, Francis Biddulph was one of twelve Staffordshire men proposed as a Knight of the Royal Oak.

TALES FROM STAFFORDSHIRE HOUSES

Maer Hall in Newcastle-under-Lyme was once owned by Josiah Wedgewood II whose Etruria works were 7 miles away. Charles Darwin proposed to Wedgewood's daughter Emma at Maer and they were married in the nearby church of St Peter. After Wedgewood's death, another pottery manufacturer William Davenport bought the house, and for most of the twentieth century it was owned by the Harrison family, of the Harrison Shipping Line.

The Wodehouse near Wombourne was the seat of landscape designer Sir Samuel Hellier and it has been claimed that the property has not been sold for over 900 years. Hellier died childless and left the property to his friend Reverend John Shaw, on the condition he would change his surname. His grandson, Colonel Shaw-Hellier, as he was known, let out the property to the Liberal MP for Wednesbury, Phillip Stanhope, and his wife Alexandra Tolstoy. Stanhope was joint president of the National League for Opposing Women's Suffrage and in 1914 was attacked with a dog whip at Euston station by a suffragette who had mistaken him for Prime Minister Asquith. Another prime minister, William Ewart Gladstone, stayed at Wodehouse on the night of 8 November 1888 after speaking at Birmingham.

Swythamely Hall, once owned by the Brocklehurst family, was brought by the World Government for the Age of Enlightenment, followers of Indian mystic Maharishi Mahesh Yogi, and was opened as a training centre for teachers of Transcendental Meditation. It was sold in 1987.

Sinai Park near Burton upon Trent has been described as 'the most important house in England to be in such a state'. The hilltop location with water supplied by a chalybeate spring suggests the potential for much earlier occupation of the site. However, the first hard evidence of habitation here are the remains of a fortified manor house in the form of the thirteenth-century moat surrounding the property and stonework in the cellars below. Sinai was donated to the monks of Burton Abbey by the Schobenhale family, and was used as a 'seyney house', i.e. a place to restore their strength after bloodletting sessions and during periods of illness – hence the name and its importance. According to English Heritage 'only a handful of similar monastic retreats or seyney houses have been identified nationally'. Sinai has surviving buildings dating to this period, which have been described as 'unique'. The three wings are structurally independent of each other and it's believed that the monks brought two medieval timber-framed buildings here from Burton, and rebuilt them parallel to each other to use as dormitories. After the Reformation, Sinai was given to the Paget family who at times used it as a hunting lodge. In 1606, they erected a medieval-style great hall to link these two wings and to impress their mates.

Sinai remained in the family for around 400 years until it was sold to pay off some of the debts run up by Henry Cyril Paget, 5th Marquess of Anglesey. The Burton and District Co-Op Society bought the property in June 1918, with the great hall, confessional, solar and chaplain's room still in evidence at the time. By the 1960s, Sinai had been converted to six cottages but, when the water supply was found to be contaminated, they were deemed unfit for human habitation. The owner, unsure what to do with this white elephant in the middle of his land, moved his pigs and chickens in. Anything that could be sold was – for example, wooden panelling went to the USA and the Tudor front door ended up at the Stanhope Arms in Bretby. At the time of writing, one wing of the timber-framed house has been restored beautifully by current owners, with another two wings awaiting salvation.

In 1972, vandals destroyed what remained of the already ruined **Handsacre Hall**. In a last-ditch effort at preservation, the surviving fragments were moved to Avoncroft Museum in Bromsgrove, where dendrochronology was used to date the timbers, giving a suggested date of around 1310, with some reused timbers from an earlier hall. The site is now a Scheduled Ancient Monument, still surrounded by a moat, 10m wide and 1½m deep, at the centre of which there is visible brick and sandstone remains.

Crakemarsh Hall at Rocester was owned by the Cavendish family. Tyrell William Cavendish, Julia Florence Cavendish and her maid Nellie Barber were passengers on the *Titanic*, on board which the former lost his life but both the women were saved. Italian prisoners of war and US troops spent time at the hall during the Second World War and it was owned by JCB during the 1970s. There is a legend that a portrait that hung in the entrance hall was cursed after two maids died after cleaning the painting. Supposedly, on the reverse of the portrait the following words were written, 'I hope whoever succeeds me at Crakemarsh Hall will cherish this portrait above all others or evil will befall them.' The painting was not sold along with the rest of the contents of the hall, remaining even when every other item of value had been stripped from the building. Eventually in 1980, someone cut the portrait from its frame. Its fate, and that of the thief, is unknown. The hall was finally demolished in 1998.

The watchtower at Hamstall Ridware was once part of the now derelict manor house, **Hamstall Hall**. When the Burton Scientific society visited, they climbed a wooden staircase to the roof where they enjoyed 'a good view of the surrounding area', and it is said that you can see four counties from the top. Other remains of the hall include a Tudor gateway. The hall belonged to the Catholic Fitzherbert family from 1517 to 1601 and Sir Thomas Fitzherbert was imprisoned in the Tower of London for thirty years until his death on 2 October 1591. In June 1939, the *Derbyshire Times* did a feature on a 93-year-old woman known as Grannie Shelton, who worked as a parlour maid and nurse at the hall. She told the paper that she had never seen a ghost but had once, 'been down amongst the dead men' – when a member of the Squire of Hamstall Hall's family died she entered the family vault to have a look around and saw six coffins inside, each covered by a black cloth but with the white face of each of the corpses visible through the glass. Mrs Shelton also once dressed up as a ghost to scare the pantry boy that she suspected of stealing fruit from the hall, causing him to run for his life shouting, 'The Devil is in the pantry!' The Devil may not have been in the pantry, but apparently he was found in a small hollow compartment in one of the bedrooms of the old manor house in the form of a stone image, complete with horns, depicted as 'shaving a pig with red skin'. The report suggests that the hall was formerly a nunnery, and this hollow would have been somewhere nuns would carry out penance for breaking the rules.

Hawkesyard Hall has been known by a variety of names including Le Hawkeserd in Hondesacre, Armitage Park, Spode House and Hawkesyard Priory. The first house known to have existed here was a moated manor owned by the Rugeley family, who appear to have had a variety of spellings for their own name. According to an article in the *Lichfield Mercury* on 3 February 1950, a document describing the funeral of Richard Rugeley, who 'departed this mortal and transitory life on Saturday night, the 5 July 1623 at his house at Hawkesyard', was signed by Symn Ruggeley, Thirkell Rugeley, Henry Rugley and Thomas Rugsley. Information on the early days of Hawkesyard is sketchy but it's thought the original hall, pulled down in 1665, was much closer to the River Trent, about half a mile to the west of Armitage Church. Nothing is thought to remain and nothing much more is known about Hawkesyard until 1760, when the estate was renamed Armitage Park by Nathaniel Lister, who built a Gothic-style mansion on the sandstone hill above the site of the original hall. Beneath Lister's new house was a plaque: 'These cellars were cut out of the rock by Richard Benton and Sons, anno Domini 1760, for Nathaniel Lister, Esq.'

From the 1840s, Hawkesyard was home to Mary Spode and her son Josiah, the fourth generation of the Stoke-on-Trent pottery dynasty, and the first not to work in the family business. Mary died in 1860, and Josiah's wife Helen died eight years later. Both are buried at St John the Baptist in Armitage, the Anglican parish church where Josiah was the organ player and warden. Despite these strong links to St John's, Josiah Spode converted to Catholicism in 1885, along with his niece Helen Gulson, who lived with him at Hawkesyard. On his death in 1893, Spode requested that Helen should continue to live at Hawkesyard until her death, after which the estate should be passed to the English Dominican Order of Friars. However, Helen decided to move out of the hall and into a cottage on the estate, allowing work on the new priory and church to begin almost immediately. Some say that this decision was inspired by a vision of the Virgin Mary appearing to Helen in the grounds of the estate, and that the altar of the new priory church of St Thomas Aquinas was supposedly erected over the site of this apparition. The Dominicans left Hawkesyard in 1988, but the earthly remains of their benefactors and some of their brethren remain. Josiah Spode and Helen Gulson are interred in a small chapel within the Priory Church, and outside in the gardens, are the simple concrete crosses marking the graves of monks.

In August 2002, notices appeared in *The Guardian*, *The Stage*, *The London Review of Books* and the *Staffordshire Newsletter*, advertising for an 'ornamental hermit' to take up residence at the Great Haywood Cliffs near the **Shugborough estate** in Staffordshire, as part of an exhibition called 'Solitude'. The Shugborough Hermit would be required to live in a tent near to the cliffs (living inside them was deemed too risky) and only had to commit to the weekend of the 21–22 September 2002. From 250 enquiries from all over the world, artist Ansuman Biswas was selected. Mr Biswas went on to spend forty days and forty nights alone in the Gothic Tower at Manchester Museum in 2009, with the aim of becoming 'symbolically dead, renouncing his own liberty and cutting himself off from all physical contact'.

The first **Ilam Hall** was built by the Port family in the sixteenth century but this was demolished by Jesse Watts Russell to make way for his much grander hall of the 1820s. On his death, it passed into the Hanbury family, but after the First World War it was too large and expensive to run and by the 1920s it was being used as a hotel and restaurant. This venture failed and most of the hall was demolished before Sir Robert McDougall bought the estate and donated it to the National Trust in 1934. Since then, the main remaining part of the hall has been used as a youth hostel and the grounds have been open to the public.

In 1961, the 21st Earl of Shrewsbury sold **Ingestre Hall** to what was then the West Bromwich Corporation. Along with the redbrick Jacobean-style mansion came sixty-six paintings, most of them portraits of the earl's ancestors – the Chetwynd, Talbot and Shrewsbury families. Amongst them are George Talbot, Keeper of Mary, Queen of Scots for fifteen years and his wife Bess of Hardwick, arguably the second most powerful woman in Elizabethan England. The 19th Earl of Shrewsbury, Charles John Chetwynd-Talbot, appears twice aged 4 and wearing a red dress, and aged around 25 wearing full dress uniform. A portrait of the infamous Anna Maria as a young woman of 17 is here too, the year in which she wed Francis Talbot and became Countess of Shrewsbury. The marriage would end with the earl's death, fatally wounded by his wife's lover, George Villiers, 2nd Duke of Buckingham, in a duel that took place on 16 March 1667. The event was recorded by Samuel Pepys who described Anna Maria as 'my Lady Shrewsbury, who is a whore, and is at this time, and hath for a great while been, a whore to the Duke of Buckingham'. There were reports elsewhere that she had attended the duel disguised as the duke's page, but whether those rumours, or the ones about what happened involving his bloodstained shirt afterwards, are true is not clear.

In 1918, William Worthington had inherited **Maple Hayes** on the Burntwood and Lichfield border from his father Albert Octavius Worthington, a partner in the Burton brewery that carried his family name, who had originally purchased the estate in 1884. However, Greville Worthington would not inherit the estate from his father. In the early hours of 17 March 1942, whilst serving as a lieutenant in the Royal Navy Volunteer Reserve at Dover, Greville drove through a restricted area. Although the sentry on duty ordered him to 'Halt!' twice, he failed to stop. The sentry opened fire and Greville was fatally wounded, dying in hospital ten days later. A verdict of accidental death was recorded. When William Worthington died in 1949, the Worthington era at Maple Hayes came to an end and, in 1950, the estate was sold. The house, and around 23 acres, were acquired by Staffordshire County Council for educational purposes. The Maple Hayes Dyslexia School has occupied the site since 1981. The remainder of the estate – some 1,500 acres, including farms, cottages and agricultural land – was sold to a trust.

The original **Elmhurst Hall** was built by the Biddulph family in the late seventeenth century and replaced by an Elizabethan-style house in 1804, with building materials from the original house being offered for sale. The second Elmhurst Hall was demolished in 1921 and its last owner was the brewer Henry Mitchell from Mitchells and Butlers brewery.

Work on the redbrick, Jacobean-style hall at **Hoar Cross** began in 1862, shortly before Hugo Meynell Ingram married Emily Charlotte Wood. The hall was completed in 1871, but in that same year Hugo was killed in a hunting accident. The widowed Emily employed George Frederick Bodley and his partner Thomas Garner to build a church in his memory, in the grounds of the home they had shared. Emily died in 1904, her remains interred near to those of her husband, whose body had been brought here from the parish church at Yoxall, after the dedication of Holy Angels in 1876. Although Emily was never completely satisfied with her creation, the church is considered a masterpiece by most. Hoar Cross Hall is now a spa resort.

Woodseat Hall was built as a home for the High Sheriff of Derbyshire in 1767. The hall was constructed by Thomas Bainbrigge and when he died in 1788, it passed to his eldest son, also Thomas. On his death, the hall passed to his daughter Elizabeth but her uncle Joseph Bainbridge contested this and began a legal battle which would run for over forty years. Elizabeth never gained control of her father's estate, which was run by trustees until 1860. In 1861, the Minton family, well-known potters from Stoke on Trent, bought the hall at auction after it had to be sold to meet the legal costs of the Bainbridge family. The Minton family sold Woodseat in 1941, after which it gradually fell into ruins. Used as a garden centre for a short time, it was eventually bought by the engineering firm JCB in 1986.

Banks' Farmhouse, once part of the Woodseat estate, was built in the late seventeenth century and was used by King Charles I as a hunting lodge. The shape of its turret gave it the nickname Mince Pie Hall.

A plot to kill the king was said to have been hatched at **Bellamour Hall** in Colton in 1679. Owner Herbert Aston, who had built the house with money raised from his friends, was incarcerated in the Tower of London along with Lord Stafford. When the plot was revealed as a hoax, Aston was released but Lord Stafford had already been executed for treason.

At Onecote, Sir Ralph de Tunstall Sneyd lived in a house called **Fairview**. During the First World War he fortified the house 'to keep the Germans out', and built a private museum and a Chapel of the Holy Grail within the house.

THE LOST VILLAGES OF STAFFORDSHIRE

Blithfield

Blore

Chartley

Chillington

Croxall

Deanslow

Freeford

Haselour

Okeover

Packington

Pillaton

Sandon

Shugborough

Statforld

Syerscote

Thorpe Constantine

Tamhorn

Wychnor

3

RELIGION IN STAFFORDSHIRE

RELIGIOUS BUILDINGS

Burton upon Trent's first mosque opened in a house on Byrkley Street in 1975 and was replace in 1977 with a purpose-built mosque on Princess Street, thought to have been the fifth oldest in the country. This was replaced by the Jamia Hanfia Ghousia mosque built on the same site in 2000.

The facade of Holy Trinity Roman Catholic Church in Newcastle-under-Lyme is built entirely from Staffordshire blue bricks and was designed by Father James Egan, the first Roman Catholic priest in the town.

Medieval floor tiles from the Barons Hall at Caen Castle are on display in the church of St Nicholas in Mavesyn Ridware.

Lady Godiva's cross in the churchyard of All Saints at King's Bromley dates back to the fourteenth century. Godiva and her husband Leofric, Earl of Mercia, had a summer residence or hunting lodge here, where Leofric died in 1057.

The building, which is now the West End Methodist Church building in Stoke-on-Trent, is a former public house, known locally as 'Corkies'.

In 1846, the owner of Rookery Farm in Cresswell discovered a wooden chest, filled with ancient vestments, behind his chimney. It's believed that these had been hidden during the Reformation and the chest and its contents were taken to the local Anglican church St Margaret's. Whilst they kept the old chest, the vestments were returned to local Catholics, which were in turn given to St Mary's Catholic church. Much of the cloth had rotted away, and much of what survived were orphreys, the heavy decorated panels attached to the vestments. Amongst them is believed to be one from Spain, brought here by Katharine of Aragon. The orphreys were restored by nuns at Oulton Abbey, one of whom decided to add her own embellishments.

St Giles at Cheadle was financed by John Talbot, the sixteenth-century Earl of Shrewsbury who lived at nearby Alton Towers. The church was designed by Augustus Pugin, and is considered to be his finest work. The earl and the architect disagreed over the expensive patterned tiles in the chancel and the Chapel of the Blessed Sacrament. Lord Shrewsbury was concerned they would be damaged by being walked upon regularly and suggested covering them with carpets. Pugin argued that this defeated the purpose of having them in the first place. A compromise was eventually reached in the form of an idea by the Clerk of Works that the tiles remained uncovered but the priest and his assistants would wear special overshoes made of cloth and Shrewsbury told Pugin, 'You may have your tiles and we shall want no carpet'.

The tiny village of Croxden is dominated by the ruins of a Cistercian abbey founded in 1176 by Bertram de Verdun of Alton Castle for the souls of his predecessors and successors. What is left of the semi-circular east end of the abbey church, unusual in England and probably inspired by the French designs the abbey's patrons would have known, lies to one side of the road that was cut through the site. The nave, south transept and other monastic buildings lie on the other. In 1288, a priest from Walsall, called William de Schepisheved, was given the task of chronicling life inside and out of these abbey walls. He worked backwards to 1066 and contemporaneously until 1320 when the entries in his hand stop, although the chronicle continues until 1374. In September 1538, Dr Thomas Leigh and William Cavendish received the surrender of the abbey and the roof was removed to prevent the abbot and resident six monks from continuing to use the site. The last Abbot of Croxden is buried at Checkley Church, alongside the tomb of the new landowners, the Foljambes, and local legend has it that his ghost haunts the churchyard in protest. Although Croxden Abbey has been privately owned since then, it has been under state guardianship since 1936, and today the ruins are cared for by English Heritage. There is a myth that the heart of King John is buried here but more reliable sources suggest that it is in fact interred at Croxton in Leicestershire.

Hednesford's first Roman Catholic priest, Dr Patrick Boyle, made frequent pilgrimages to the shrine at Lourdes in France. Conscious that many in the diocese were unable to visit themselves, he conceived the idea of bringing the experience of Lourdes to them, but died long before the thirteenth-century-style church of Our Lady of Lourdes and its replica grotto were completed in 1934. Due to mining subsidence in the area, the concrete church is built on an adjustable concrete raft.

The Nanaksar Gurdwara Temple was opened in 1972 when the Sikh community of Stafford purchased the parish hall of St John's Church, originally built as the St John the Baptist Mission Church in 1902.

Completely rebuilt by the Victorians in 1842, the church of St James in Pipe Ridware was deemed surplus to requirements by the Church of England in 1983, and has since been used as a community theatre.

A twelfth-century font at the church of the Holy Cross in Ilam is thought to tell the story of the Anglo-Saxon St Betram, patron saint of Stafford, who is buried at the church here.

St Mary's Church in Tutbury originated as a Norman Benedictine friary and its west doorway is one of the best examples of Romanesque sculpture in the county.

The font at St John the Baptist in Armitage is an example of early Romanesque carving, possibly an example of Norman design and Saxon workmanship, and has been described by the Corpus of Romanesque Sculpture as being the finest and most alien medieval carving in the county.

According to Pevsner, the church of St Lawrence in Gnosall features some of the most exciting Norman work in the county. Here be dragons and other fantastical creatures, Saxon and Scandinavian influences, a green man and other ancient faces.

The Wat Mahathat Buddhist Temple at King's Bromley is based in Eastfields House, a former Victorian gentleman's residence.

St Giles is the patron saint of lepers and surely it's no coincidence that there was a medieval hospital at nearby Freeford, caring for those unfortunates suffering from the disease. Less readily explicable is the short-lived name change at the end of the nineteenth century when, according to the Whittington History Society, the church was known as St Matthew's for around twenty years, before reverting back to St Giles in the 1890s. The only original part standing today is the base of the tower, with the nave being rebuilt in 1761 following a fire and the chancel added in the 1880s. The Jacobean oak pulpit, installed here in 1922, was originally donated to Lichfield Cathedral in 1671. One hundred and eighteen years later it was moved to St Peter's at Elford but was discarded when that church was renovated in 1848 and lay disused in the stables of Elford Hall until a new home was found at St Giles. In the north and south windows of the chancel, there are fragments of medieval painted glass thought to originate from the Benedictine abbey at Burton.

The aforementioned hospital for lepers at Freeford was dedicated to St Leonard and, in 1917, around eighty skeletons were discovered in a field known as the 'Chapel Yard'. One of the skeletons was holding a chalice and patten, suggesting that they were the mortal remains of a priest. Further remains were uncovered in 1969. The hospital appears to have fallen into disuse by the late fourteenth century.

Workmen discovered the foundations of an ancient chapel beneath the lawn at Bellamour Lodge along with a carved stone head, which is now preserved in the village of Colton. A number of human bones were discovered on the same site, suggesting that this may have been an ancient burial ground.

In the 1860s, the entrance to the crypt at St Editha's in Tamworth was via a trapdoor and narrow passage, although nowadays the crypt is accessible via a flight of steps. One theory is that 700 years ago the crypt was part of a standalone chapel, which may even have been Saxon in origin. Beneath the floor of the crypt is a plague pit and there are coffin lids in the roof. At some point in the fourteenth century it was incorporated into the main church and during the reign of Elizabeth I it was used as a charnel house to accommodate the old bones that were disturbed when new graves were being dug in the churchyard. This remained its purpose until 1869, when the crypt was needed to house a boiler and the bones were returned to the churchyard, reburied in the north-east corner. When Charles Ferrers Raymond Palmer entered the crypt, the bones were stacked up in very regular order and occupied the whole of the east end, where local folklore had it that a passageway ran from here to the castle. In trying to find this passageway, Ferrers says he made a path through the bones by 'carefully piling them aside' but found 'nothing there, except the remains of the ancient altar; the stone slab of which is gone'. He was unable to examine the floor at the base of the altar as there was nowhere to store the bones, which were 'so rotten, that they crumbled to pieces beneath our feet' as 'in spite of all our efforts, they returned to our feet, and their dull clatter seemed a reproach to us, for disturbing their long and quiet repose in the sacred place'. A Latin inscription thought to date back to the fourteenth century is still visible on the wall of the crypt and translates as:

O Lord of wealth and power
Thou shalt not live for evermore
Do well whilst life thou hast
If thou should live when death is past

With the population rising in the early nineteenth century the old parish church of St Augustine's in Rugeley was outgrown and a new one was built on land opposite. Consecrated on 21 January 1823, the new church was built on land belonging to Viscount Anson, the cost met from a variety of sources. According to some, stone from the nave of the old church was sold off to raise funds, leaving just an arcade of arches to connect the fourteenth-century tower with the old chancel. In the 1970s, the church yard was landscaped and the gravestones which once surrounded the church were broken up and used to pave what was once the nave and north aisle, creating a mosaic of carved names and epitaphs belonging to the old inhabitants of Rugeley.

Although largely rebuilt in the nineteenth century, St Peter's Church at Elford is famous for its medieval monuments. The most well known is the 'Stanley Boy', said to depict young John Stanley, last of the male line, holding a tennis ball in his left hand, and pointing to the place where it fatally hit him with his right. However, in an article for the Church Monument Society, expert Sophie Oosterwijk dates the monument as thirteenth century whereas, according to the story, John Stanley died in around 1460. It has also been suggested that at some point the effigy may have been modified to add weight to the local legend. Dr Oosterwijk suggests that the monument may in fact have been a miniature effigy, erected to mark a medieval heart burial, where the organ was buried separately to the rest of the body.

The Trentham Mausoleum was built to be the final resting place for members of the Sutherland family and is Stoke-on-Trent's only Grade I listed building.

The tower of St Chad's in Lichfield houses four bells. Three of them were cast in the seventeenth century and the oldest of these three dates to 1625 with the inscription 'DOMINO CANTICUM CANTATE NOVUM'. The second is from 1664 and declares 'GOD SAVE THIS CHURCH AND REALM THE KING IN WAR, I.C.1664'. Even the latest of the three, featuring the names Ralph Low and Richard Grimley, is from 1670 meaning that the people of the parish and those who are passing by have heard these same bells ring out for well over 300 years. The fourth bell is even older still, featuring an inscription that reads, '+O BEATE MARIAA.A.R', and some numerals that no one has been able to read. An article in the *Lichfield Mercury* in August 1936 describes it as 'England's Oldest Bell', giving it a date of 1033, but this is far from proven.

When the present church of St John's at Shenstone was built in the 1850s, the existing church was only partly demolished, leaving the remains of the tower and the south door still standing in the churchyard.

St Bartholomew's in Farewell was once the site of a Benedictine nunnery. The place name refers to the 'pure or clear' spring that still flows here. The original church incorporated material from the nunnery, but much of it was demolished and rebuilt in brick in the 1740s. Three rows of different sized earthenware vessels were discovered in the south wall of the church at the time of the renovations. The jars were found lying on their sides, their openings facing inside the church, covered with a thin coat of plaster. Sadly most were broken during the work but one of the jars found its way to Mr Greene's Museum of Curiosities on Market Street, Lichfield, although its whereabouts is now unknown. The purpose of the jars remains a bit of a mystery. The accepted explanation is that they are 'acoustic jars', and as the name suggests, were used to improve the acoustics in the church, based on a theory from a Roman architect called Vitruvius. However, others have suggested that they may be related to the idea of votive offerings.

A document described as an 'indenture chirograph', 2ft 5in long and 11in wide, lists the goods found in the sacristy of Lichfield Cathedral in 1345. The first part of the inventory lists the various relics owned by the cathedral, including, of course, those of St Chad. Other relics recorded include some of Mount Calvary and Golgotha, a piece of the rock upon which Jesus stood and wept bitterly, some of the bones belonging to the Eleven Thousand Virgins, part of the finger and cowl of St William, some of the bread of St Godric and some of the wood from the cross of St Peter. There were also said to be some of St Lawrence's bones, part of his tomb and a piece of the gridiron he was executed on, and at No. 23 The Close different coloured bricks have been used on the south wall to depict this symbol of the saint's martyrdom.

In 1803, the Reverend John Kirk built a new chapel dedicated to St Peter and St Paul in Upper St John Street, Lichfield. Due to religious sensitivities, the chapel was originally designed to look like a dwelling house, but in 1834 a turret and a new entrance was added, and the name changed to Holy Cross. St Peter and St Paul was the dedication later given to the city's second Roman Catholic church, opened on 29 June 1967.

The church of St Lawrence in Rushton Spencer is known as 'the chapel in the wilderness' due to its isolated location.

Amidst the other burials and baptisms of the parish register of St Lawrence in Gnosall, an interesting entry appears on an otherwise blank page. At some time between 20 March 1684 and 19 April 1685, an unknown hand has written the following:

> Fere god and honour the King
> Honor your parents at all times
> Wimins tongues air like [unfinished]

Keele University Chapel is the first religious building in the country designed to accommodate services for different Christian traditions and was consecrated by the Anglican, Roman Catholic and Free churches. George Pace originally designed the building to be faced with sandstone but when the Berry Hill Brick Company donated industrial-style bricks to the university, the chapel was instead constructed from these Staffordshire blue bricks. In protest against government cutbacks to education expenditure, the words 'No Cuts' were painted on the roof of the chapel. It's said that the graffiti artist, who may or may not have been a member of the university hang-gliding club, forgot to take a paintbrush and so the letters were daubed on with a rolled up sock.

When the early-sixteenth-century tower at St John the Baptist Church in Mayfield was completed by Thomas Rollestone in 1515, he added the inscription *Ainsi et mieux peut etre*, which translates to something like 'Thus it is and better it could be' and appears to be a variation on the Rollestone family motto. Some have interpreted this as an indication that Thomas thought he could have done a bit of a better job on the tower. The door to the tower is peppered with holes and the story goes that on 7 December 1745 the retreating army of Bonnie Prince Charlie passed through Mayfield, murdering an innkeeper and a man who refused to hand over his horse before turning their muskets on the church door, behind which the terrified villagers had barricaded themselves.

St Giles at Newcastle-under-Lyme, rebuilt on medieval foundations by Sir George Gilbert Scott, is the only twelve-bell tower in north Staffordshire and is frequently used by teams practising for national competitions.

St James in Barton-under-Needwood, the only church in Staffordshire to be built in the Tudor period, stands on the site of the cottage where founder Dr John Taylor was born in *c.* 1480, the eldest of triplets. The story of the Taylor triplets is well known although several versions exist. In perhaps the most romantic of these, King Henry VII was hunting in Needwood Forest when he was separated from his companions. He stopped off at a small cottage to seek directions back to Tutbury Castle and found that the couple living there were the parents of three strong healthy triplets. Perhaps a more likely story is that three surviving triplets were presented to the king as, if not quite by miracle, something that may have appeared close to one in those days when between a third and a half of children didn't make it to their fifth birthday (the king would himself go on to lose three children in their infancy). What is certain is that Henry took it upon himself to be responsible for the boys' education. In John's case, there is note in the Royal Privy purse expenses of 1498 'for the wages of the King's Scoler John Taillor at Oxenford'. A career in the Church and as a civil servant followed, with John eventually holding the position of Master of the Rolls between 1527 and 1534. It may sound like he was in charge of the king's packed lunches but it was actually the third most senior judicial position in the country. Taylor's initials can be found on the church tower alongside the year 1517, when work commenced at St James (then dedicated to Mary Magdalene). Work was completed in 1533, and Taylor died the following year. However, his final resting place is elsewhere. John Stow's survey of London in 1598 records it as being at St Anthony's Hospital in London. However, there is a suggestion that the intention was for it to be here at St James, which would have brought the local lad-done-good's life full circle. Pevsner suggests that a blank arch in the north wall of the chancel may have been designed to house his tomb although why this never came to be is unknown.

Five Bishops of Lichfield are buried at Holy Trinity in Eccleshall, including William Overton (1525–1609) who was responsible for bringing French glassmakers to the area, with furnaces set up in the nearby Bishop's Wood and James Bowstead (1801–43), the former Bishop of Sodor and Man who became the Bishop of Lichfield in 1840. Extra information given on a card in the church includes the curious story that his mother's grave states that she once prophesised that James would become the bishop of two sees. In the choir vestry, relocated from the chantry, is the tomb of Thomas Bentham (1513–78) who became the first Bishop of Lichfield under Elizabeth I as well as the first bishop to marry. John Lonsdale (1788–1867), the last Bishop of Lichfield to live in Eccleshall Castle, has a commemorative tablet on the south wall of the chancel and is buried in the churchyard here although he also has an effigy in Lichfield Cathedral. I'm also assuming that Robert Wright, the bishop who died at Eccleshall Castle in September 1643 and whose burial was delayed as the castle was under siege from the parliamentarians, was eventually laid to rest somewhere here too. Over in the Old Baptistry is the tomb of Bishop Richard Samson (*c*.1470–1554) who gained favour with Henry VIII thanks to his support for the king's divorce from Catherine of Aragon.

On April Fools' Day 1990, a former churchwarden climbed the spire at St Mary's in Uttoxeter to highlight the appeal to replace a third of the spire, which had been removed the previous year on grounds of safety. On spotting an undertaker in the crowd, which had gathered to witness her climb, she joked, 'Pine with brass handles please'. The spire had been rebuilt after being struck by lightning in 1814 and on its completion, two chambermaids at a local hotel climbed up to kiss two of the stonemasons. The events were captured in a rhyme: 'Maggy the maid, in a moment of bliss, Ventured her neck for a sweetheart's kiss, Higher and higher she ascended the spire, Till she reached the top stone and attained her desire.'

A thirteenth-century bronze seal from the priory at Stone was discovered in a field in Cobham in Surrey, and after local people raised £8,000 it was returned to the town and is now on display in the church of St Michael and St Wulfhad.

St Mary's at Patshull is closed and is now cared for by the Churches Conservation Trust.

BURIALS AND MONUMENTS

The neo-Egyptian-style mausoleum erected for the Marquis of Stafford, later the Duke of Sutherland, opposite Trentham Gardens is Stoke's only Grade I listed building. It was built in 1807/08 to house the remains of members of the Leveson-Gower family, although these were removed in 1907 and buried elsewhere in the cemetery.

It was the custom of the Dyott family of Freeford Hall to be laid to rest in the family vault at St Mary's Lichfield at night, following a torchlit procession from their home Freeford Hall, accompanied by servants and workers from the estate. On such occasions, crowds would line the route of the cortege in order to witness the eerie spectacle. The last of the Dyotts to be buried in this fashion was Richard Dyott, former MP for Lichfield. When the procession arrived at the church in the Market Square at 10 p.m., the doors to the church had to be closed to prevent crowds from entering and newspapers across the country reported 'disgraceful scenes' of 'wild excitement', with one report even suggesting that one of the police officers in attendance had almost had his fingers bitten off during the fracas.

The oldest headstone in the county, possibly the country, is found in the churchyard at Alstonefield and belongs to Anne Green who died in 1518.

When extension work was carried out at Checkley Church, eight bodies were found in a 2ft square area. Their arms and legs had been removed in order to allow as many burials as possible. The remains were dated to around AD 1320.

The Marquess of Donegall was buried in a mausoleum at the church of St Michael's in Lichfield but did not rest in peace for long. Rabbits found their way into the coffins, and then restoration work in 1842–43 saw the family mausoleum go the same way as the family home, Fisherwick Hall, which had been demolished earlier that century. According to the church booklet, the present location of Donegall's remains is unknown.

Two Egyptian mummies, brought to Tamworth in the 1930s by the Reverend William MacGregor, are buried in the foundations of the former Palace cinema in the town. The mummies were originally interred in the back garden of MacGregor's home Bolehall Manor but were relocated after they began to deteriorate.

Inside All Saints' Church at Grindon, there is a memorial to those who lost their lives when their Halifax Bomber crashed on the nearby moors as they attempted to deliver supplies to the villages of Grindon and Butterton, which had been cut off by snow on 13 February 1947. Halifax RT922 attempted to land twice but was unable to locate the cross made of soot, indicating the landing site. On their third attempt, the starboard wing clipped the ground and the bomber crashed to the ground, killing all eight crewmembers on board. Even more tragically, the roads to the village were reopened the very next day. A 6ft-high cairn marking the site of the crash on Grindon Moor was erected in 1999.

Within the walls of the mausoleum, in the churchyard at St Michael's and St Wulfhad in Stone, lie the remains of the town's most famous son, Admiral John Jervis. He was born in January 1735, at Meaford Hall, entering the Royal Navy at the age of 13. On St Valentine's Day 1797 he defeated the Spanish fleet off Cape St Vincent and as a result was created Earl St Vincent, after the cape off which the battle was fought. When one of his best seamen lost his life savings whilst swimming, Jervis gave him the money from his own pocket. Jervis died at the age of 88 on 23 March 1823, in Essex, and was interred in the Jervis family mausoleum at 4 p.m. on Wednesday 26 March 1823.

In January 1873, there was a fire at the Breadmarket Street premises of a Lichfield clock- and watchmaker. Three generations of a family lost their lives and their bodies were laid out on the pavement before being taken to the guildhall where a

Catholic priest read the burial rites. The family were then taken directly to the graveyard at St Michael's where the Reverend J. Sejeantson carried out a burial service. Three monuments to the family members can be found at Holy Cross RC and the middle stone carried the inscription, 'Refused admission into St Michael's Churchyard'. The tragedy led to the council taking over the responsibility for fire fighting in the city, buying an engine and establishing a brigade, with a building in Sandford Street being used as a fire station.

William Billinge, buried at the church of St Bartholemew in Longnor was born in 1679 and died at the age of 112 in 1791, having served at Gibraltar and Marlborough before being sent home wounded. When recovered, he defended the king in the Jacobite uprisings. The epitaph on his gravestone tells the story of his life as follows:

> In memory of William Billinge, who was born in a corn field at Fawfieldhead in this Parish in the Year 1679. At the age of 23 years he enlisted into His Majesty's Service under Sir George Rooke and was at the taking of the Fortress of Gibraltar in 1704. He afterwards served under the Duke of Marlborough at the ever-memorable Battle of Ramillies, fought on 23rd May 1706 where he was wounded by a musket shot in the thigh. He afterwards returned to his native country and with manly

courage defended his Sovereign's rights at the Rebellion in 1715 and 1745. He died with a space of 150 yards of where he was born and was interred here the 30 January 1791 aged 112 years. Billeted by Death I quartered here remain. When the trumpet sounds I'll rise and march again.

In 1960s, archaeologists working at the Spital Chapel of St James in Wiggington discovered a shallow grave containing the remains of a woman and two children, despite the area never having been consecrated as a burial ground. How or why the skeletons came to be buried here is still a mystery.

In the 1970s, the remains of a decapitated male missing several bones were discovered at Hulton Abbey. Analysis at the University of Reading indicated that the man had been hung, drawn and quartered. In 2008, the body was identified as being that of Hugh Despenser the Younger, a favourite of Edward II. When Isabella and Roger Mortimer deposed Edward in 1326, Despenser was sentenced to death as a traitor, and on 24 November 1326 he was roped to four horses and dragged through the streets to the walls of his own castle where a gallows had been constructed. A man sliced off his penis and testicles, flinging them to the fire below, and then cut out Despenser's heart and entrails. The corpse was then decapitated. The head was sent to London whilst Despenser's arms, torso and legs were sent to be displayed about the gates of Newcastle, York, Dover and Bristol. Hugh's wife had asked for her husband's bones to be returned to her for burial on the family estate in Gloucestershire but only the head, a thighbone and several vertebrae were returned to her. These are the bones missing from the skeleton at Hulton Abbey, which formed part of the estate owned by Despenser's brother-in-law, Hugh Audeley.

Singing Kate was an Italian governess employed by Francis Biddulph at Rushton Grange. Her nickname arose from her beautiful singing voice. Kate contracted plague in 1647 and Francis rode through the village looking for a doctor, unknowingly spreading the disease wherever he went. The plague victims were buried in a pit near Rushton Grange, which is known to this day as Singing Kate's Hole.

A fourteenth-century tombstone belonging to Richard the Merchant is embedded into the wall of The Friary at Lichfield, one of the earliest Franciscan buildings in England.

A tomb in the graveyard of the Old Chancel in Rugeley belongs to two women: Elizabeth Cuting who died in 1695 and her sister Emma Hollinhurst who passed away a year later. Effigies of the sisters tied into their burial shrouds are carved on top of the tomb. An information board nearby tells how this unusual monument gave rise to a local legend that Oliver Cromwell, despite dying in 1658, had buried the women alive in sacks. The true story of the tomb relates to an Act of Parliament, which required corpses to be buried in wool. The burial register shows that these ladies along with others defied the Act and were buried in linen.

Craven Kynnersley of Loxley Park was accidentally shot in the thigh when his greyhound knocked the trigger of his gun. A stone obelisk in the grounds of the hall marks the incident.

Thomas Meakin, buried at Rushton Spencer, was first buried at Stone. When his pony began to paw the grave his friends opened it and found the body lying face down indicating that Thomas had been buried alive.

In the medieval period, the Lollards, followers of fifteenth-century religious reformer John Wycliffe, used a ravine near Gradbach as a secret place of worship to avoid persecution by the Catholic Church. Lollards were considered heretics and burned for their beliefs. Lud's Church may have been named after Walter de Ludank, or Lud Auk, who was captured attending a Lollard meeting there. Walter's daughter, Alice, was tragically shot during a raid on a religious service; her ghost is said to haunt the chasm. A wooden ship's figurehead from the ship *Swythamley* was placed in a high niche above the ravine by the local landowner Philip Brocklehurst, to commemorate Alice and it came to be known as 'Lady Lud'.

In the churchyard of St Margaret's at Wolstanton is the headstone of Sarah Smith who died in 1738 aged 21. The stone includes a short poem written in the first person in which Sarah suggests that she was murdered, even giving a clue to who did it:

It was C_ s B_w that brought me to my end
Dear Parents mourn not for me
For God will stand my friend
With half a Pint of Poyson
He came to visit me
Write this on my Grave
That all that read it may see.

In the Market Square in Lichfield there are plaques commemorating three martyrs who were burned at the stake here in the reign of Queen Mary. They were Thomas Hayward and John Goreway, executed in September 1555 and Joyce Lewis from Mancetter who was burned on 18 December 1557. Another plaque commemorates Edward Wightman who was the last person in England to be burned for heresy on 11 April 1612.

The mausoleum of Chancellor Thomas Law in the graveyard of St Michael's, Lichfield, originally incorporated a clock illuminated by gas so that people travelling along the road to Burton upon Trent and Lichfield Trent Valley Railway station could tell the time.

In the churchyard of St Edward's at Leek, the gravestone of James Robinson suggests he lived to the miraculous old age of 438.

However, as he died on 28 February 1788, it seems likely that the stonemason got carried away, adding an eight to the end of the numbers.

When Sir John Egerton, supporter of the Royalist cause during the civil war, was buried at St Werburgh's Church in Hanbury, his sister chose to bury him in the north aisle of the church, far from the busts of two Puritan ladies, Katherine Agarde and her daughter Ann Wollcocke. The church is also home to the tomb of Sir John de Hanbury, the oldest alabaster monument in Staffordshire dating to around 1303.

One of Lichfield Cathedral's best-loved monuments is Sir Francis Chantrey's 'The Sleeping Children', also known as the Snowdrop Monument, which commemorates two sisters, both of whom died tragically young. It was commissioned in 1816 by their mother, Ellen-Jane Robinson, who wanted to remember her daughters asleep in each other's arms. Chantrey left an uncarved piece of marble on one of the girl's feet, as he believed only God could create perfection. Ellen-Jane later paid for the construction of Christ Church in the Leomansley area of the city and she is buried here alongside her third husband Richard Hinckley and her son from her second marriage, Hugh Woodhouse Acland, who also died tragically young and was the first person to be buried in the graveyard of the new church.

RELIGIOUS LEADERS

Edmund Gennings from Lichfield was executed during the Reformation for being a Catholic priest. He was hung, drawn and quartered in London on 7 November 1591 and it is said that whilst he was being disembowelled the hangman said, 'Zounds! See, his heart is in my hand and yet Gregory is in his mouth. O egregious Papist!', after hearing Gennings say, '*Sancte Gregori ora pro me*'. On 25 October 1970, Gennings was one of the forty martyrs of England and Wales canonised by Pope Paul VI.

Dame Eleanor Davies, a fervent anti-papist, believed she was a prophet and that she could predict events in England based on anagrams she found in the Bible and specifically, the Book of Daniel and Revelation. She even managed to create an anagram from her own name – 'Reveal O Daniel' – which she considered evidence of her gift (although this form of prophecy was later mocked when at one of her trials it was discovered that another anagram of her name was 'Never Soe Mad a Ladie'). At Michaelmas 1636, Eleanor was staying in Lichfield but moved from The Angel pub into the cathedral close to live with Susan Walker. Eleanor, Susan, and another local woman called Marie Noble, were said to have spent a lot of time discussing religion and went every day to the cathedral to protest against the seating arrangements which gave priority based on social rank and office, by sitting in the seats reserved for gentlewomen and the wives of the bishop, dean and canons. According to Esther Cope's biography, there is no record of what specifically led Eleanor and the other women to protest but we do know that Eleanor wrote to the bishop to express her disapproval about whatever it was. When no reply was received, she took her protest to the next level, sprinkling the new altar hangings at the cathedral with a mixture of tar, pitch and puddle water and sitting on the bishop's throne where she declared herself 'primate and metropolitan'. On hearing of this, the Privy Council ordered that she be sent to Bedlam without trial, although Eleanor actually remained here in the city until mid February, as the messengers bringing the order were delayed by bad weather. According to Cope, both Susan Walker and Marie Noble were also later prosecuted for 'discussing religion'.

Accepted Frewen was nominated by King Charles I to be the consecrated Bishop of Lichfield, but as a result of the Civil War, never actually set foot in Lichfield Cathedral.

In around 1794 Louis Martin de Laistre, a French émigré priest who fled from the revolution, came to Mucklestone. He was the first of such priests to settle in Staffordshire and for a time tutored the children of the rector, later taking charge of the Catholic mission at Ashley.

George Fox, founder of the Society of Friends, known as the Quakers, visited Lichfield shortly after his release from Derby Gaol in 1651. After seeing the spires of the cathedral, Fox removed his shoes, leaving them with some shepherd. He walked a mile barefoot into the centre of the city, and went up and down the streets and into the market place crying, 'Woe to the bloody city of Lichfield!' Fox believed he saw a channel of blood running through the streets and a pool of blood in the market place. Eventually, he was approached by a friendly group of people who asked, 'Alack George! Where are thy shoes?' Fox attributed his vision to the story of the thousand Lichfield Martyrs from the time of the Emperor Diocletian. This memorable visit is recorded on a plaque on St Mary's Church in the Market Square.

Hugh Bourne and William Clowes were the founders of Primitive Methodism. Bourne was born at Bucknall in 1772 and at the age of 27 he joined the Wesleyan Society at Burslem. Clowes was a Burslem man and despite early ambitions to be the premier dancer in the country, he converted to Methodism in January 1805. An open-air camp lasting fourteen hours was held at Mow Cop on the Staffordshire–Cheshire border in 1807, and as a result of this and subsequent meetings, Bourne and Clowes were expelled from the Wesleyan church. The separate movement became known as Primitive Methodism and the first chapel was built in Tunstall in 1811. Bourne had it built like a row of houses so that if the movement didn't take off, the building could be sold for residential use. However, it thrived and today there are over 4,000 Primitive Methodist chapels across the country.

The initials 'A.D.' can be found carved into the end of a medieval bench at Checkley Church. They belong to Anthony Draycot, once Rector of Checkley and later chancellor to the Bishop of Lichfield at the time of Mary I. Draycot is described in Foxe's Book of Martyrs as being 'cruel and cold'. During this time, Draycot was responsible for sentencing Joan Waste, a 22-year-old blind woman from Derby, to be burned at the stake for heresy. Joan's crime was to have bought a New Testament, which she paid friends to read to her, a penny at a time. At the Diocesan Court in Lichfield, Joan argued that she could no longer understand mass as it was said in Latin and could not accept that a priest's blessing could change bread and wine into body and blood. Waste's public execution took place on 1 August 1556 at Windmill Pit off the Burton Road in Derby, where she was hanged over a fire until the rope burned through. A memorial to Joan Waste can be found in the otherwise unrelated Birchover Church. On the day of the execution, Draycot is said to have given a sermon before going home to eat. After refusing to take the oath of supremacy when Elizabeth I came to the throne, Draycot was stripped of all ecclesiastical offices, other than the rectory of Draycot, and condemned to the Fleet Prison as 'an irreconcilable Papist' from 1560 until the last year of his life when he was allowed to return to Paynsley Hall, the family home at Draycott in the Moors. A memorial can be found at the church of St Margaret's in the village.

SEVEN STAFFORDSHIRE SAINTS

St Werburgh was born near Stone in the seventh century and was the daughter of the Mercian King Wulfhere and St Ermenilda. Her uncle King Ethelred I founded a nunnery at Hanbury where Werburgh became prioress. When she died at Trentham Priory around AD 700, her body was initially there but was later stolen by the people of Hanbury who had built a shrine for her. With the threat of Danish invasion looming, it was deemed wise to move the remains of the saint to a fortified place where they could be better protected. Chester Cathedral was chosen and when they came to move the body they found the remains perfectly preserved. The journey to Chester took five days and Werburgh became the patron saint of the city. Of the many miracles attributed to Werburgh the most famous is that of the flock of geese stolen and killed by a servant, which she brought back to life. As a result, she is often symbolised by a flock of geese.

St Modwena arrived in the area now known as Burton upon Trent in the seventh century and built a chapel on the Andressey Island, where she would heal disease. Legend says she cured a prince who would later be known as King Alfred the Great.

St Chad was appointed by King Wulfere to be the first Bishop of Lichfield and to spread Christianity throughout Mercia. After only two and a half years, in AD 670, Chad died of plague and he was buried at what was to become Lichfield Cathedral. From the thirteenth century, his body was enshrined in a tomb behind the high altar, which in the thirteenth century was decorated with statues and precious jewels and his skull was kept separately in the Head Chapel in a painted wooden case. After the Reformation, Chad's relics were smuggled out of Lichfield and went on a journey of 30 miles that took 300 years. In 1837, they were transferred to the new Catholic cathedral of St Chad in Birmingham, where they were interred in a new shrine designed by Augustus Pugin. In 1985, the bones were examined and although it was discovered that there were three femurs, they were dated to the seventh century and authenticated as true relics by the Vatican. St Chad's feast day is celebrated on 2 March.

It was reported that during the disputed election in Florida in 2000, visitors to the website of St Chad's Church in Lichfield, where the saint once baptised converts, had increased from an average of 4 a day to around 300 as American voters searched the internet for more information on the fragments of paper created when ballot cards are punched, also known as Chads.

St Betram, an Anglo-Saxon prince, travelled to Ireland to seek guidance from St Patrick and whilst there met an Irish princess and bought her back to Mercia. Whilst travelling through the Moorlands, the princess gave birth in a cave. Whilst Bertram was out hunting for food his wife and child were killed by wolves. The grief-stricken Bertram renounced his royal heritage and asked for a piece of land to build a hermitage on the Isle of Bethnei, later to become Stafford. In his later years, Bertram spent time in a cave in Ilam where he died and he is buried in the church of the Holy Cross.

St Editha was the sister of Athelstan, the King of Mercia who would later unite Saxon England. In an attempt to broker peace with the Danes who controlled Northumbria, Editha was betrothed to Viking King Sihtric. However, within a year he had abandoned Christianity and his new wife, who became the prioress at Polesworth Abbey.

St Ruffin and St Wulfhad were two legendary Saxon princes murdered in AD 665 by their father Wulfhere, pagan King of Mercia, after he discovered they had converted to Christianity. Their mother, Queen Ermenilda, buried their bodies beneath a heap of boulders at a place now known as the town of Stone and later built a church on the site. This original church was destroyed by Danes in the ninth century and was replaced by an Augustinian priory in 1135. The present church of St Michael and St Wulfad in Stone was built in the 1750s using stone from the priory.

4

STAFFORDSHIRE SPORT

THE BEAUTIFUL GAME

When the whistle blew at the end of the FA Cup final between Birmingham City and West Bromwich Albion on 25 April 1931, rather than celebrating with his own team mates, Birmingham keeper Harry Hibbs ran the length of the pitch to shake hands with the opposition goalie Harold Pearson, a good friend and fellow Tamworthian.

Albert Brown, born in Tamworth and reputed to be the fastest sprinter in English football, was nicknamed the 'Tamworth Sprinter' and played for Southampton in the FA Cup final of 1902. The Saints were playing Sheffield United, which included 20-stone goalkeeper William Foulke, nicknamed 'Fatty'. The referee, a Staffordshire man called Kirkham, awarded Southampton a controversial equaliser just before the final whistle, enraging the Blades' keeper. After the game ended in a draw, Foulkes raced naked from the changing rooms to argue with the referee about his decision, who locked himself in a cupboard to escape. Brown scored in the replay, but Sheffield won the cup.

On his debut for Birmingham City in 1980, Tamworth-born goalkeeper Tony Coton saved a penalty.

Liverpool and England international player Daniel Sturridge attended the Friary School in Lichfield.

At the end of the nineteenth century, Hednesford Town Football Club played at the recreation ground at the Lodge, given the nickname 'The Tins' in reference to the metal sheeting which surrounded the ground. The club fell into debt, which a local councillor agreed to pay off provided the team move to a patch of land behind the Cross Keys Inn. Having outgrown their Cross Keys ground in the 1990s, the club moved to a new stadium called Keys Park, opened officially by Sir Stanley Matthews before a match against Wolverhampton Wanderers.

The ashes of Sir Stanley Matthews are buried beneath the centre circle at Stoke's Britannia Stadium. Matthews was the first footballer to be knighted; he also won the first European Footballer of the Year title. He retired from professional football in 1965 at the age of 50, having never been booked throughout his entire career.

By December 2009, Burton United FC were nineteen points clear at the top of the Blue Square National Conference. Promotion to the Football League seemed guaranteed and Blue Square, who sponsored the league, declared Burton to be champions and paid out on all relevant bets. However, promotion began to look less assured as their lead began to ebb away. Promotion came down to the last game of the season, with Cambridge United just three points behind them. Burton lost to Torquay but fortunately for the Brewers, Cambridge also lost, earning Burton Albion a place in the Football League for the first time since 1907.

In January 1985, Burton Albion played Leicester City. Gary Lineker put Leicester in front but after the Brewers equalised, goalkeeper Paul Evans was struck on the head by a piece of wooden seating. With no substitute keeper, Evans had to play on. Leicester went on to win the match 6–1, but after a Football Association review it was decided that the game should be replayed as a result of Evans' injury. The replay took place behind closed doors at Highfield Road, Coventry, with Leicester winning 1–0.

Port Vale played Charlton on Boxing Day 1932, but the match was abandoned due to thick fog. Vale's Jimmy Oakes had played in the original match but by the time the game was replayed the following April, he had signed for Charlton, making him the first player to play for the opposing club in a rearranged match. It could be said he was the first player to play for both sides in the same game.

Bobby Charlton played his last football league game against Port Vale in March 1975 when he was player manager for Preston.

Port Vale were included as a team in the 'Rest of the World' section after supporter Robbie Williams agreed to provide an original theme tune for FIFA 2000 on the condition that his team featured in the game.

The training regime for Port Vale during the 1953/4 season was a run from Burslem to Hanley and back with a stop at a pub for half a shandy.

Part of Archie Maxwell's transfer fee from Darwen to Stoke City was a set of wrought-iron gates for the Lancashire club's ground.

Stoke were one of the twelve founder members of the Football League along with Preston North End, Aston Villa, Wolverhampton Wanderers, Blackburn Rovers, Bolton Wanderers, West Bromwich Albion, Accrington, Everton, Burnley, Derby County and Notts County. The League's office was at 8 Parkers Terrace, Etruria.

During the 1889/90 season, Stoke City lost 10–0 to Preston, and this remains their worst League defeat to date.

In the third round of the Birmingham Junior Cup between Robirch Athletic and Bass & Co., played at Branston, no ball was available at the start of the match. The referee had to send a request to the Branston Artificial Silk Football Club to borrow theirs so that the game could be played. Eventually, Bass & Co. won 7–2.

Jack Evans was the first player to be sent off for Stoke City, in a game against Everton in November 1892.

During the second leg of a cup final tie between Stoke and Bolton on 9 March 1946, overcrowding in the ground caused what is now known as the Burnden Park Disaster. Thirty-three fans were killed and 400 injured. Incredibly, the match was restarted with a sawdust touchline separating the players from the bodies of those who lost their lives that day.

Stoke City were the first Icelandic-owned football team outside of Iceland.

When the roof of the Victoria Ground's Butler Street stand was blown off in a gale, Stoke City's home game against Middlesbrough had to be played at Port Vale's ground Vale Park. Making the necessary repairs to the roof landed Stoke in financial difficulties and players had to be sold to cover the costs.

In 2006, former Arsenal and England player Paul Merson joined Tamworth under an arrangement that his previous club Walsall, where he had been player-manager, would continue to pay his wages. The arrangement lasted just two games. Merson played in both and, after suffering a 5–0 defeat in the second, announced his retirement from professional football.

The training ground at St George's Park has a replica of the Wembley surface.

Stoke's final game at the Victoria Ground was against West Bromwich Albion, the team who had been their first ever opponents when the Football League began in September 1888.

Burton Albion's Pirelli stadium is on the former site of the Italian tyre firm's sports and social club.

Names and Nicknames

Ambitious plans for Vale Park in the mid twentieth century led to it being described as 'The Wembley of the North'. However, by 1950 there were still temporary dressing rooms and the ground remained uncovered.

Stoke City FC were originally known as Stoke Ramblers but changed their name when city status was granted to the town in 1925.

Hednesford Town FC are known as the Pitmen, in reference to the town's mining heritage.

Unofficial Port Vale fanzines include 'The Memoirs of Seth Bottomley', the 'Vale Park Beano', and 'Derek, I'm gutted!', with the latter inspired from a remark made by former manager Brian Horton to journalist Derek Davis, following a defeat to Tranmere Rovers.

The origins of the name Port Vale are unclear. One theory is that the club was created at a building called 'Port Vale House'. Others suggest the name comes from a canal wharf near Burslem.

CRICKET

Sydney Barnes, once described as 'the greatest bowler that ever lived', was an inaugural member of the International Cricket Council (ICC) Cricket Hall of Fame in 2009. Originally working as a clerk at a Staffordshire colliery, he later worked for Staffordshire County Council where he became a skilled calligrapher and presented Queen Elizabeth II with a handwritten scroll to mark her visit to Stafford in 1957. Barnes died at his home in Chadsmoor, Cannock, in 1967.

David Steele, a former English International cricketer, was born in Bradeley. On his debut against Australia at Lords in 1975, he found himself lost in the basement of the pavilion having gone down too many flights of steps. Steele was voted BBC Sports Personality of the Year in 1975, and one of the Wisden Cricketers of the year in 1976. He also persuaded a butcher in Northampton to reward him with a lamb chop for each of his first fifty runs, and a steak for each run thereafter.

Bob Taylor from Stoke holds the first-class record for 1,649 dismissals in 639 games. When in the hospitality tent at Lords during the 1986 Test match against New Zealand, he was persuaded to come out of retirement and take to the field when England's wicket keeper was hit on the head. Taylor played for the rest of the day wearing an assortment of borrowed kit although he did wear his own gloves, which he had in his car.

ATHLETICS

Joe Deakin from Shelton lead the British team to victory in the 3-mile team race at the 1908 Summer Olympics. It is claimed that the winning time was actually faster than the 14 minutes and 39.6 seconds recorded, but British timekeepers had been so excited by the result they forgot to stop their watches as he crossed the finish line. A celebratory lunch of steak and champagne followed, and in the afternoon Deakin lined up for the heats of the 5-mile race, but perhaps unsurprisingly failed to finish. Deakin continued to compete until his ninetieth birthday, still able to run a mile in under 10 minutes, and died three years after his last race. A trophy presented to the winner of a veterans' road race to celebrate Stoke-on-Trent's 100th birthday was named in his honour.

Field hockey player Imran Sherwani from Stoke-on-Trent won gold with the Great Britain squad at the 1988 Summer Olympics in Seoul, scoring two of the three goals in the final against Germany. Sherwani was one of the torchbearers for the 2012 Olympic torch relay.

Angela Smith, born in Stoke-on-Trent, was the first female squash player to turn professional. Smith was both British and World Champion and only lost twice whilst playing for the country. She began as a tennis player, swapping sports after constant rain during her tennis season.

Peter Thornley from Stoke-on-Trent is better known as retired professional wrestler Kendo Nagasaki. In the year 2000, at a ceremony at Victoria Hall in Hanley, he accepted the Wrestler of the Millennium trophy.

Captain Matthew Webb, the first man to swim the English Channel, in August 1875, hosted his First Grand Aquatic Entertainment at Rudyard Lake in June 1877, which included a miniature demonstration of his historic swim in front of over 25,000 people. The shops and factories in the area were closed for the occasion, which also included a man and dog swimming race, Miss Agnes Beckwith (Champion Lady Swimmer of the World) and a demonstration of a rescue from drowning by two talented swimmers. Spectators were assured that bathing costumes would be full and complete, ensuring that even the most fastidious of either sex could be present with propriety at the event.

On 7 August 2016, Adam Peaty from Uttoxeter won Great Britain's first medal of the Olympic Games in Rio de Janeiro for the 100m breast stroke. Peaty also broke the world record, which he himself had set the previous night! He was the first British male to win an Olympic gold for swimming for twenty-eight years. As a boy, Peaty had a phobia of water and would scream when his parents tried to bathe him.

GENERAL SPORTING TRIVIA

The playing of tennis, handball and bowls was banned in Tamworth in the fifteenth century.

Singer Robbie Williams was once junior captain of Burslem Golf Club, opened on 28 September 1907 by Scottish music hall star Sir Harry Lauder.

Phil 'The Power' Taylor, born in Burslem, Stoke-on-Trent, is considered the best darts player of all time having won 214 professional tournaments, including eight consecutive World Championships between 1995 and 2002.

Hednesford Hills Raceway was built inside an old reservoir about 1 mile outside the town in 1952 and is a quarter-mile length oval. As well as stock car, hot rod and banger racing, the venue has also hosted double-decker bus and combine harvester racing.

5

SCIENCE, INDUSTRY AND INNOVATIONS

THE LUNAR SOCIETY

The Lunar Society was a group of industrialists and intellectuals who met during the late eighteenth century to explore ideas and conduct experiments on the night of the full moon each month. Although the society was largely based in Birmingham, several of its members had Staffordshire connections.

One of the founder members was **Erasmus Darwin,** a physician, philosopher, poet and inventor who hosted Lunar Society meetings at his home on Beacon Street in Lichfield and formed the Lichfield Botanical Society, comprising him and two other men.

Eight Inventions by Erasmus Darwin
A speaking machine
A canal lift for barges
Darwin designed a horizontal windmill and convinced Josiah Wedgewood to install one at his Etruria Works, where it operated for thirteen years before being replaced by a Boulton and Watt steam engine
A carriage that would not tip over
A steering mechanism for his carriage, adopted by cars 130 years later
An artificial bird
A copying machine
Several weather monitoring machines

Other Lunar Society Members

Matthew Boulton was an engineer and co-founder of the Lunar Society, along with Darwin. Boulton's family were from Lichfield, his father moved to Birmingham in the early eighteenth century. When Boulton married distant cousin Mary Robinson, they lived in Lichfield with Mary's mother before themselves moving to Birmingham when Matthew was made a partner in his father's toy-making business. From 1766 to 1809, Boulton lived at Soho House alongside the mill he transformed into his Soho Manufactory.

John Whitehurst was a Derbyshire-based clockmaker and pioneer of geology.

Josiah Wedgwood was born in Burslem and is credited with the industrialisation of the manufacture of pottery at his Etruria Works factory alongside the Trent and Mersey Canal, a scheme that he had been a great supporter of and heavily involved in. Wedgewood's daughter and Darwin's son were the parents of the naturalist Charles Darwin.

Dr William Small was professor of Natural Philosophy at the College of William and Mary in Williamsburg, Virginia and later involved with planning and building Birmingham General Hospital, though he died of malaria before it was completed in 1779.

Richard Lovell Edgeworth was an inventor who lived at Stowe House in Lichfield for a time. Whilst living in the city he met two of his four wives, Honora Sneyd and her sister Elizabeth, who he married three years after Honora's death.

James Watt was an inventor and engineer who improved the efficiency of Newcomen's steam engine and entered into a partnership with Matthew Boulton in 1775. Both men appear on the £50 note. Amongst Watt's significant contributions to industry is the development of the concept of horsepower, and his name is of course known to all as the unit of measurement for the rate of energy conversions.

James Keir was a chemist and geologist who leased and managed a glassworks at Amblecote near Stourbridge, before giving it up to run Boulton and Watt's engineering works at Soho. Keir studied the mineralogy of Staffordshire and contributed an article on it to Stebbing Shaw's *History of Staffordshire*. Keir also wrote a memoir of his friend and fellow Lunar Society member, Thomas Day.

Thomas Day was an author best known for the children's book *The History of Sandford and Merton* and his infamous and failed experiment to train a perfect wife.

Dr William Withering was a former physician at Stafford General Infirmary where he met his wife Helena Cookes, a botanical illustrator. Whilst collecting specimens for her to draw, Withering's interest in botany developed and he compiled several works on the subject. However, Withering's most famous discovery was the role that foxglove could play in the treatment of heart conditions, as described in his 1785 work *An account of the Foxglove and some of its Medical Uses*.

Joseph Priestly was a clergyman and scientist, who invented soda water and is often credited with the discovery of oxygen.

Samuel Galton Jnr was a Quaker gunmaker who held several of the society's meetings at his home in Great Barr, Birmingham.

OTHER STAFFORDSHIRE INNOVATORS

Robert Bage established a paper mill at Elford and together with his friend Erasmus Darwin, and others, he opened an ironworks and slitting mill at Wychnor. When this business folded, Bage began a career in literature, writing six novels over fifteen years. Bage was an enlightened employer, caring for the welfare of the workers at his mill and he was a trustee of the Reverend Hill's charity, helping to provide an education for the poor children of the village.

Sir Jonathan Ive, a former pupil of Walton High School in Stafford, is the chief design officer of Apple Inc. In 2004, the BBC named him the Most Influential Person in British Culture, and in 2008 he was named the Most Influential Briton in America, with the *Guardian* describing him as the 'Inventor of the Decade' in 2009. Ive's innovations include the iPod, iMac, the iPhone and iPad.

Thomas Mayer and his son, also Thomas, established the county's first veterinary surgery in Newcastle-under-Lyme in around 1813. Mayer Senior died in 1835 and his grandson Thomas Walton Mayer joined the family business. In 1884, Mayer Junior and his son campaigned for the Charter of the Royal College of Veterinary Surgeons, and with it the recognition that it was not a trade but a profession, with the title of Veterinary Surgeon restricted to qualified practitioners.

Clarice Cliff, born in Tunstall on 20 January 1899, spent three years at the Burslem School of Art and obtained a job at A.J. Wilkinsons of Burslem. The company, seeing her talent, allowed her to experiment with her own designs and bought the neighbouring Newport Pottery Works to act as a base for her work. One of her first ranges was called 'Bizarre', which consisted of bright colours and geometrical shapes. It proved so popular that more staff were taken on, who became known as the 'Bizarre Girls'. Queen Mary was not a fan, describing Clarice's designs as 'awful'. As the Second World War broke out, most of the factory's workforce was drafted into the armed forces and production ceased. Clarice retired in 1939 but will be remembered as a prolific art deco ceramic designer.

In 1688 the **Elers brothers** from Holland, both potters by trade, established a pottery factory at Bradwell near Burslem after discovering fine red clay there. Their products were stored around a mile away at Dimsdale, and the two sites were reportedly connected by a speaking tube. As a way of protecting their commercial it's said that secrets the Elers employed the stupidest workers they could find, but were eventually tricked by John Astbury who gained access to their works. On learning the Elers brothers' trade secrets he set up a rival establishment at Shelton. Astbury is credited with being the first Staffordshire potter to use flint for improving the quality of earthenware mixture, after seeing it being used at a tavern to treat a horse, which was going blind.

On an archaeological dig in Japan, Scottish missionary **Dr Henry Faulds** noticed the fingerprints of ancient craftsmen impressed onto clay, and after gathering further samples from his students came up with the theory that they were unique to each individual and could therefore be used as a means of identification. A break-in at the Tokyo medical centre, where he was working, gave Faulds the opportunity to put his theory to the test, when he cleared the name of a falsely accused colleague by comparing his fingerprints to those left at the scene. Faulds published a letter on his findings in *Nature* magazine and contacted Charles Darwin who passed on the information to his cousin Francis Galton, who along with William Herschel would later be given credit for proposing the forensic use of fingerprinting. Faulds moved to Staffordshire where he worked as a GP and a police surgeon in Hanley and Longton before retiring to Wolstanton, where he died in March 1930, bitter that he had never been properly credited for his work. However, in recent years, Faulds' contribution to the science of fingerprint identification has been recognised: with a plaque honouring his work in the village as well as a forensics laboratory named after him at Keele University.

PUMPING STATIONS OF STAFFORDSHIRE

The Edwardian **Mill Meece Pumping Station** near Stone is believed to be the last surviving example of an intact twentieth-century water-pumping station. Water was pumped from four boreholes by two steam engines on the site to a reservoir in Hanchurch to supply the Potteries. The steam engines were in use until 22 December 1979. Electric engines still pump water from the site but the horizontal steam engines, which were used up until December 1979, have been preserved and are now looked after by the Mill Meece Preservation Trust.

Sandfields Pumping Station is a Grade II* listed Victorian works, with its original 190hp Cornish beam engine still *in situ* – the only surviving one of its kind in the world. Sandfields was built by the South Staffordshire Waterworks Company to pump water from the city of Lichfield to the Black Country during the time of the cholera epidemics of the mid nineteenth century. In 1997, the company ceased abstraction at the site and the building became redundant. An on-going campaign by the Lichfield Waterworks Trust to save Sandfields and its unique engine for the community is currently in full flow.

The mock Tudor **Brindley Bank Pump House** at Rugeley was opened by the South Staffordshire Waterworks Company in 1905 and contains a horizontal tandem compound engine made by Hathorn Davey of Leeds.

Milford Waterworks was built in 1890 to supply water to Stafford and the surrounding area from reservoirs located on the Satnall Hills.

Cresswell Pumping Station opened in July 1932 and contained a pair of triple-expansion vertical steam engines, two of the last steam engines to be installed in the country.

Claymills Pumping Station was built in 1885 to deal with the problem of sewage in the town of Burton-on-Trent, and ran until 1971. In 1993, a trust started work to restore the engines and to transform the site into a museum and visitor attraction. Claymills is described as Britain's most complete example of a Victorian sewage pumping station and is home to the oldest working steam-driven dynamo in the country.

Maple Brook Pumping Station in Burntwood is a Grade II listed building built by the South Staffordshire Waterworks Company between 1912 and 1915 and is one of the few remaining pumping stations with original triple-expansion steam engines still *in situ*.

The **Bratch Pumping Station** was built by Bilston Urban District Council in 1895 to provide an independent supply after a dispute over costs with the Wolverhampton Corporation which had been supplying the town with water.

Horns Pool or Dutton's Pool behind the Horns Inn dates back to the 1620s and was the pond for what is thought to have been the first slitting mill in the Midlands. Iron arriving here from forges in north Staffordshire was split into rods using the power of water. The mill was pulled down in 1932 to make way for the **Slitting Mill Waterworks**, owned by the South Staffordshire Waterworks Company and one of the first pumping stations to be powered by electric, rather than steam. On demolition of the mill, the *British Numismatic Society Journal* noted that,

'An uncertain number of coins, said in one report to date from the seventeenth century, and in another to be of both that and the following century were found "in the walls".'

MILLS, MINES AND FACTORIES

A hole covered by a sliding shutter discovered at Tean Hall Mill may have been a 'breast hole', allowing women workers to feed their babies when they were brought to the hatch by carers at lunchtime. Although the mill has been redeveloped this feature has been retained.

Siemen Bros Electrical Engineering Works relocated to the Lichfield Road in Stafford from Woolwich in 1903 along with 800 employees, manufacturing generators, electric motors and electrical appliances. However, as a German-owned company, the factory was taken over by the government during the war and afterwards merged with several other companies to form the English Electric Company.

Armitage Shanks was founded in 1817 in the village of Armitage as a 'sanitary pottery manufacturer'. Armitage Ware Limited merged with rival company Shanks Holdings Limited in 1969. The company is one of the sponsors of the Loo of the Year Award.

The Branston Artificial Silk Company producing rayon started in 1927, at the former Branston Pickle factory in the village. The buzzer that signalled the start and end of the working day could be heard across Burton upon Trent.

Wire manufactured at Bolton's Copper Works at Froghall and Oakamoor was used in the first transatlantic telegraph cable.

The Gladstone Pottery Museum in Longton, is a complete example of a Victorian pot bank, taking its name from a visit by the British Liberal politician and four-time prime minister

who visited Burslem in 1863 to lay the foundation stone of the Wedgewood Memorial Institute. There are less than fifty surviving bottle ovens across Stoke-on-Trent.

In 1793 Thomas Minton established a pottery factory in Stoke-on-Trent producing earthenware and, later, bone china. When Minton died, his son Herbert took over the firm and branched out into new fields, including the production of decorative encaustic tiles. Between 1844 and 1858, Herbert Minton donated tiles to forty-six Staffordshire churches and parsonages.

In 1937 Chatterley Whitfield became the first British mine to reach the singular production milestone of one million tons of coal in a single year, and north Staffordshire could boast the greatest increase in output per man shift in the country.

In 1945 Joseph Cyril Bamford founded JC Bamford Excavators Limited in Uttoxeter, now known as JCB. The firm, based in the nearby village of Rocester, is the world's third-largest construction equipment manufacturer. The firm's first vehicle was a tipping trailer made from war-surplus materials, which J.C. Bamford built in a rented lock-up garage in Uttoxeter.

The Bamford family had previously started Bamfords, later Bamford International Farm Machinery, which was a large employer in the town from the end of the nineteenth century through to the early 1980s when it gradually went into decline before closing in 1986.

In the 1870s John Key owned a draper's business in Rugeley where his son George set up his own business. In 1888 George developed a new kind of coat for the navvies working on the Manchester Ship Canal, made from a thick, hardwearing material. The coat became known as the donkey jacket, after the 'donkey engines' which some of the navvies worked on.

In the 1990s medieval glass furnaces were excavated near to Rugeley. In 1419, much of the glass produced there was sold to York Minster where it was painted and used in the windows of the chancel.

Since 1961, a coal-fired power station has operated alongside the River Trent at Rugeley. Rugeley 'A' station had five towers, the first of which to be built was used by the RAF to help develop parachute technology. Coal was supplied directly from the nearby Lea Hall Colliery until it closed in 1991, and 'A' station itself was demolished in 1995. Rugeley 'B' power station opened in 1970, and whilst both stations were operational around 850 people were employed. Decommissioning of the 'B' power station began in June 2016 and demolition of the site is due to take place before summer 2019.

In 1877, a young sculptor called Robert Bridgeman came to Lichfield to work on the restoration of the cathedral. Using a small shed near to Minster Pool as a workshop, Robert produced more than half of the statues that now grace the magnificent west front of the cathedral. Bridgeman would eventually become one of the biggest employers in Lichfield. In 1968, Charles Bridgeman sold the firm to Messrs F. and E.V.

Linford, building contractors of Cannock, on the understanding that Bridgeman & Sons would be a subsidiary of the larger firm, retaining not only their name and employees but also their Lichfield premises. Sadly, in October 2011, Linford-Bridgeman went into administration.

Many people believe the Trotters drove around Peckham in a Reliant Robin in *Only Fools and Horses* but it was actually a Reliant Regal van. Tom Williams founded the company in 1935 and for many years, Reliant was Tamworth's largest employer and also the second largest British car manufacturer between the 1960s and 1990s. In September 2000 the company announced that no more of the three-wheeled vehicles, for which they were famous, would be made after February 2001. To mark the end of an era, sixty-five special edition Robins with gold paint, leather trim and a walnut dashboard were manufactured to celebrate sixty-five years of production and the last Robin was collected on 14 February 2001. That was not the end of the Robin, however. On 30 April 2001, the company moved to Cannock and B&N Plastics started production of a Robin BN-1 after buying the manufacturing rights. The names lives on in Tamworth where the site of the old factory is now a housing estate called Scimitar Park, with road names such as Tom Williams Way, Regal Close and Robin Close.

Several examples of nailers' stones can be found in the churchyard of Christ Church in Burntwood, and are believed to have been used in the local nail-making cottage industry. Workers would take their products to the nearby Star Inn, where they would be weighed and paid for by middlemen who would also replenish their supplies of iron.

On 1 September 1871, the Fair Oak Colliery Company acquired a sixty-year lease on 5,500 acres of mineral rights lying beneath the surface of Cannock Chase, but the company had failed to

sink any boreholes in the area to test the geology. Work on the two shafts of the No. 1 Plant immediately hit trouble, as dynamite was needed to blast through layers of sand and gravel and water had to be pumped from the shafts. The stone extracted from the shafts was used as stepping-stones across the nearby Stony Brook and in the dam walls of the pools at Fairoak. The plant was abandoned in 1875, having failed to yield a single ton of coal. However, the company's second attempt was more successful and the No. 2 plant began to produce coal in 1877, producing around 2,000 tons a week and employing almost 400 people. However, the early problems continued to blight the company's finances and mining operations ceased less than ten years later.

Production at the East Cannock Colliery, near to the former Globe Inn in Rugeley, began in 1876 when two shafts were completed – one named 'Amy', after the daughter of the company chairman. The following year, an explosion of methane killed four boys and four horses, seriously injuring two men. Each of the injured men was awarded £10 10s and the owner of one of the horses received £15 15s. The company was in liquidation by 1880 and was sold for £20,000 to a Welsh businessman. The colliery was taken over by the National Coal Board in 1947 but closed ten years later.

At Chatterley Whitfield Colliery on 7 February 1881, a fire caused by the misuse of an underground blacksmith's furnace resulted in an explosion, killing twenty-four men and boys. An inquiry into the disaster was held at the Norton Arms public house, and at the Stafford Assizes Manager Edwin Thomas was acquitted of manslaughter.

At Diglake Colliery, Audley near Newcastle-under-Lyme, seventy-eight miners lost their lives when water from an old flooded pit gushed into the lower area of the mine. Some of the bodies were never recovered and the mine was never reopened.

Staffordshire's worst mining disaster was at the Minnie Pit at Halmer End, Newcastle-under-Lyme, on 12 January 1918, when it is believed a faulty safety lamp caused an explosion of gas and coal dust, leading to the deaths of 155 men and boys. Of these, 144 were poisoned by carbon monoxide and 11 were killed by the impact of the explosion. The captain of the mine rescue team was killed during the rescue attempt and due to the presence of gas in the mine it took over a year for all of the bodies to be recovered. There had already been two explosions at the mine. On 6 February 1898, a blast had killed all the pit ponies and nine miners were killed on 17 January 1915. The pit was closed in April 1930 and a memorial to those who lost their lives was erected by the National Coal Board and Audley Rural Parish Council in January 1981.

On Saturday 25 November 1911, two underground explosions at the Jamage Colliery at Talke, Newcastle-under-Lyme, killed six men and injured fourteen others. Twenty-seven pit ponies also died in the disaster and others were rescued after being trapped underground for twenty-one days.

Fred Barrett, a coal miner and pit collier from Hanley, took a job on RMS *Titanic* as a lead stoker in boiler room 6, the site of the collision with the iceberg. As the water began to pour in, Barrett managed to escape into boiler room 5 and eventually escaped the sinking ship on Lifeboat 13, which he took charge of for an hour before the cold rendered him incapable. Barrett and the others were rescued by RMS *Carpathia* at 4.45 a.m.

CANALS

The Harecastle Tunnel on the Trent and Mersey Canal at Kidsgrove is, in fact, two separate tunnels known as Brindley and Telford. The former was of course built by James Brindley between 1770 and 1777, and at the time was one of the two longest canal tunnels in the country – the other being at Norwood on the Chesterfield Canal. It is said that on Brindley's birthday, the sunrise is aligned with the entrance to the tunnel. The latter was built by Thomas Telford and was completed in 1827 after three years of work. After part of it collapsed from subsidence in 1914, the Brindley tunnel was closed and since then only the Telford tunnel has been open, taking around thirty minutes to travel along its 2,675m passage.

The Bratch Locks on the Staffordshire and Worcestershire Canal is a flight of three separate locks, designed by James Brindley, which originally took the form of a three-lock staircase.

The Cannock extension of the Wyrley and Essington Canal was completed in 1863 and supposedly so many barges used to leave the basin at noon each day that they created a small bore which ran the whole length of the canal.

Rudyard Lake was formed in 1799 by the Trent and Mersey Canal Company as a reservoir to feed the Caldon Canal through a canal feeder emanating from south of the lake fed with water from the Dingle Brook and the Rad Brook.

In December 1830, the *Staffordshire Advertiser* reported on 'The Navigator's Funeral'. James Wheeler was helping to cut a tunnel for the Shropshire Canal through the solid rock when he fell to the bottom of Cowley Quarry in Gnosall and later died of his injuries. His colleagues – 100 of them – each contributed one shilling to ensure he had a decent burial, and when they discovered his coffin had already been nailed shut demanded the lid be removed to check nothing was amiss. Six of the men were under bearers and the wives of six men supported the pall. Six overseers of the works followed as chief mourners and behind them came 100 fellow navigators, two abreast. The report noted that whilst the mourners were not wearing black, they were decently attired and looked clean and respectable. The women wore their brightly coloured clothes and the men wore smock-frocks. During the burial, some of those assembled at the graveside expressed anxiety about the security of the corpse and assisted the sexton in filling up the grave. Afterwards, the mourners held a wake at the Roe Buck and the *Advertiser* expressed sorrow that many of them had stayed out until late and 'finished up the solemnities of the day with a fight'. However, the journalist also commended the navigators for their praiseworthy practice of not only subscribing towards the funeral expenses of their colleagues but of also clubbing together something out of their wages every week to support the sick amongst them.

UP IN THE AIR

Lichfield is associated with the world's first ever long-distance air race. The challenge, first issued by the *Daily Mail*, offered a prize of £10,000 to the first pilot who flew from London to Manchester with less than two stops, in under twenty-four hours. Claude Grahame-White took off just after 5 a.m. on 23 April 1910. About 115 miles into the journey a problem with the engine forced him to land in the field 4 miles outside of the city. The farmer charged the crowd of spectators admission but soldiers from nearby Whittington Barracks kept them from getting too close to the plane. Unfortunately, it was the soldiers themselves who caused the most damage to the plane by ignoring Grahame-White's instructions to peg it down securely, allowing it to be blown over and damaged. Together with his stricken craft, Graeme-White took a train back to London from Lichfield Trent Valley rail station to prepare for another attempt. In the meantime, his rival, Paulhan had taken off from London at 5.30 p.m. on 27 April, and he too had been forced to make a landing in the Lichfield area after running out of fuel.

After pegging down his craft in a field near Trent Valley railway station, from where his rival had set back off to London with his plane tail between his legs, he headed to the city's George Hotel, intending to restart at 3 a.m. At 5.32 a.m. Paulhan landed at Barcrioft Fields near Didsbury, and took the prize. Grahame-White was forced to land at Streethay, on the outskirts of Lichfield, and abandoned his attempt.

During Burton Aviation Week, held from 26 September to 1 October 1910, flags were flown from the Waterloo Tower to signal to the crowds gathered on Bass Meadows whether flights had been suspended due to wind or whether another flight was imminent. Due to high winds, nothing much happened on the first day of the show. On day two, however, things got very exciting, and not just for people gathered on Bass Meadows. News had reached Lichfield that some of the pilots would be flying around the cathedral in an attempt to win a cup given by the Marquis of Anglesey for the fastest round trip. Large crowds assembled around Minster and Stowe Pools, in the cathedral close (it was even reported that there were people up the central spire) and on the Burton Road. At 5.15 p.m., Julien Mamet whirred into sight on his Bleriot plane, swept around the north side of the cathedral, flew south over Christ Church and the bowling green and headed back for Burton where he arrived fourteen minutes later. There was a lot of cheering and waving of hats and hankies (what would we wave nowadays? Nothing probably, we'd be too busy trying to record it on our phones). An hour later, a shout went up as another Bleriot, this time piloted by Paul de Lesseps, was spotted. The *Mercury* reported that although de Lesseps lost his bearings by following the wrong train line somewhere around Wychnor Junction, he managed to find them again, approaching the city from the south and flying parallel to Bird Street above the heads of the crowd.

By this time it was dusk and de Lesseps, deciding he would be unable to reach Burton before dark, landed his aircraft in a field belonging to Grange Farm on Wheel Lane, clipping the tail on a fence (it was later reported that de Lesseps had only narrowly missed the roof of the farmhouse). As darkness fell back at Bass Meadow, the mood changed from excitement to concern. Mamet had flown up to meet his rival, but saw no sign of him. As spectators lit bonfires, flares and lamps in the hope they would guide de Lesseps safely back to Burton, a search party set off in the direction of Lichfield. Eventually, they found de Lesseps in the field, signing scraps of paper by matchlight for a crowd of autograph hunters. The damaged plane was taken charge of by the police, and de Lesseps was taken to the George Hotel, where he informed a crowd gathered at the steps that he hoped to fly back to Burton at 4 p.m. the following day, once he had made the necessary repairs. Well, that was the plan anyway. Flying back to Burton, however, in an attempt to break the record for flying at high altitude, de Lesseps missed the town altogether. There was another anxious wait for the crowd who had seen de Lesseps flying over at a great height before disappearing in the direction of Derby. Eventually, a message was received that he had landed safely at Colwick Hall near Nottingham.

De Lesseps' return journey to Burton was also not without drama. As he flew over Meadow Lane, where Notts County were playing Bristol City, he caused such a sensation that the match had to be stopped for a few minutes as the crowd, players and officials gazed upwards. Unfortunately, the referee, a Reverend Marsh, forgot to adjust his watch, blew his whistle four minutes too early and had to call the players, some of whom had already started to get changed, back out of the dressing rooms to finish the match.

Reginald J. Mitchell was born in Kidsgrove and educated at Hanley High School. In 1917, Mitchell joined the Supermarine Aviation Works at Southampton and between 1920 and 1936, designed twenty-four aircraft, including record-breaking seaplanes and the iconic Spitfire. Despite battling cancer, Mitchell continued to work on the aircraft that would play a crucial role in the Battle of Britain, although he sadly died of cancer just a year after his iconic aircraft first took to the skies. To celebrate the connection with Mitchell and the Potteries, Spitfire RW388 was donated to Stoke-on-Trent in 1972 after use as a training aircraft and as part of a gate display at RAF Benson and RAF Andover. Mitchell was awarded the CBE in 1932 for his contribution to high-speed flight and, in 2003 was picked as the Greatest Midlander in a BBC vote. His former school was renamed Mitchell High School in 1989 and a statue of him stands outside the Potteries Museum and Art Gallery in the town.

Thomas Lister of Armitage Park near Rugeley was a novelist and the first Registrar General for England and Wales. Lister was responsible for setting up the system of civil registration for births, deaths and marriages as well as organising the 1841 census, the first in which every individual would be named as well as counted. Lister died of tuberculosis in 1842 before the results from what is known as the first modern census had been collated.

RAILWAYS

Sandon station was built in 1849 for guests visiting Sandon Hall, home to the Earl of Harrowby, and has a covered entrance to protect the earl from the rain. The station closed in 1955 and is now a private residence.

The Bolebridge Railway viaduct in Tamworth was officially opened on 4 August 1839 when George Stephenson drove an engine called *Tamworth* over it.

The North Stafffordshire Railway line is known as 'The Knotty'.

Only three original stations on the Churnet Valley branch line of the North Staffordshire Railway survive. These are:

Alton Station, built in 1849, and used by the Earl of Shrewsbury who had a suite of waiting rooms inside the three-storey tower and a luggage lift to hoist his baggage to the entrance of Alton Towers. Renamed Alton Towers in 1954, after the estate it served, it is the only Italianate station on the line and was closed in 1965. The stationmaster's house and the waiting room are now owned by the Landmark Trust and are rented out as holiday accommodation.

Cheddleton Station, built in 1849 and reputedly designed by Pugin, has been home to the Churnet Valley Railway and North Staffordshire Railway Museum since the mid 1970s. The station was almost demolished in 1974, but a member of Cheddleton Parish Council parked his car in front of the builders, buying time until the authorities could arrange for the building to be protected.

Rushton Station, now a private residence, was opened in 1849.

The now redundant Leek Brook Station was largely used as an interchange with the St Edwards Hospital Tramway, operated by Staffordshire County Council who purchased an electric locomotive from Wolverhampton and a London horse tram to transport both passengers and coal to the hospital. Passenger services were discontinued in the 1920s but coal deliveries continued until 1954.

The Grand Junction Railway is carried over the River Penk by a viaduct with seven arches, each one 37ft high and 30ft wide.

During the First World War, the two military camps set up on Cannock Chase were served by the Tackeroo Railway, which had been built to transport supplies and equipment to the camps. It ran from the main line at Milford to the West Cannock No. 5 Colliery and the train running on the line became known as the Tackeroo Express.

In January 1968, the intercity Manchester to London express hit a low-loader transporter on an automatic crossing at Hixon. Eleven people were killed and forty-five were injured.

The London to Manchester and the Liverpool to London intercity services collided at Colwich Junction near Rugeley on 19 September 1986, killing the driver of the Liverpool to London train and injuring seventy-five others.

FIVE STAFFORDSHIRE ENTRIES IN THE *GUINNESS BOOK OF RECORDS*

The record for the largest gathering of fairies is held by St Giles Hospice, Whittington, after 871 participants took part in the Solstice Walk on 22 June 2013.

The longest scream by a crowd was recorded at Drayton Manor Theme Park near Tamworth on 12 April 2014 and lasted 8 minutes 45 seconds.

On 7 August 2014, the record for the largest gathering of scarecrows in one location (3,812) was awarded to the National Forest Adventure farm near Burton upon Trent.

When Louie May jumped out of a balloon at 3,352m above Longton, on 9 June 1908, her ripcord jammed. Dolly Shepherd, another member of the performing troupe taking part in the feat, brought her down on her single chute, the first mid-air rescue recorded.

Four members of the Staffordshire Ambulance Service hold the record for the longest marathon CPR session. Two teams of two, made up of Ray Edensor and Emma Parker, and Paul Gauntlett and Mark Brookes, spent 151 hours at the Asda superstore in Stafford between 19 and 25 January 2004, carrying out cardiopulmonary resuscitation, consisting of fifteen compressions alternating with two breaths.

STEPHEN SUTTON

When Burntwood teenager Stephen Sutton was diagnosed with terminal cancer he drew up a bucket list of things he wanted to achieve before he died. One of those things was getting in the *Guinness Book of Records* and on 4 May 2014, Stephen joined another 553 people at his former school, Chase Terrace Technology College, to achieve the record for the most people making a heart-shaped hand gesture at the same time. Another record followed on 10 July 2015 at Hibaldstow Airfield, when 402 people made 4,013 tandem jumps in twenty-four hours in Stephen's honour, beating the previous record of 286. By the second anniversary of Stephen's death on 14 May 2016, over £5.5 million had been raised for the Teenage Cancer Trust, services to which he was awarded an MBE for in May 2014.

6

FOOD AND DRINK

STAFFORDSHIRE SPECIALITIES

Marmite
In 1902, the Marmite Food Extract Company was formed in Burton upon Trent, after German scientist Justus von Liebig found that brewer's yeast could be concentrated and eaten as a separate foodstuff. Yeast was supplied by Bass Brewery. The name derives from a French word for a large cooking pot, and the paste was originally sold in earthenware pots, but since the 1920s, Marmite has been supplied in glass jars with a picture of the pot on the label. During the First World War British troops were issued with Marmite as part of their rations, as the spread is a good source of vitamin B and folic acid. Its health benefits have also been used to treat anaemia in mill workers in Bombay in the 1930s and malnutrition during a malaria epidemic in Sri Lanka in the 1930s.

Playing on the strong reactions to the product's distinctive flavour, the company launched its 'Love it or Hate it' campaign in 1996, and the phrase the 'Marmite effect' made it into the English language. In 2002, to celebrate the company's 100th birthday, employees were given a limited edition gold jar in a commemorative box and Vivienne Westwood designed an anniversary t-shirt.

An urban legend suggests that Marmite is banned in British prisons as it can be used to make alcohol. There were reports in

2009 that Marmite Mule was a speciality at Dartmoor Prison, but a spokesman for the prison service denied it was banned stating that it was not possible to make alcoholic drinks from the paste.

Pointons Sweets

Willian Henry Pointon came to Hednesford from Tipton to work as a miner but one of his hobbies was making sweets and so he opened up a stall on Hednesford Market. By 1890, he had opened a shop on the Cannock Road, where they continued to make their own sweets until the 1950s. At its peak, the business had sixty sweet rollers, fifteen machines and five copper boilers operating two days a week and producing around 700 weight of sweets on average. The bestsellers were Horehounds, made from an herbaceous plant grown on William's allotment, and Pink Ones, made using aniseed. The business still trades today, although it is now purely wholesale and locals still refer to the business as 'Sucky Pointons'.

Hovis Bread

The brand originated in 1886 when Richard 'Stoney' Smith, born in the Millhouse at Stone, developed a way of extracting the wheatgerm from flour, cook it lightly without destroying the nutrients and returning it to the flour. The process was patented in 1887 and known as 'Smith's Patent Germ Flour'. Smith joined with a company of Macclesfield millers, Fitton & Sons Ltd and in 1890,after a nationwide competition for a more appetising name was held, the company became known as The Hovis Bread Flour Company, a portmanteau word of the Latin phrase *hominis vis* meaning 'strength of man'. Stoney is buried in Highgate Cemetry in London, beneath a monument which tells his story.

Another flour-related claim to fame for Staffordshire is that the steam-powered Coton Mill on the Shropshire Union Canal in Gnosall is supposedly the place where self-raising flour was invented.

Oatcakes

Although non-locals refer to them as Staffordshire oatcakes, residents of north Staffordshire simply call their local delicacy oatcakes, although nicknames include the 'Tunstall Tortilla' and the 'Potteries Poppadom'. Many producers prefer to keep their exact recipe secret, but the basic ingredients are oatmeal, flour and yeast mixed together and cooked on a griddle. In the Potteries, oatcakes were often sold from the window of a house; the 'Hole in the Wall' in Stoke-on-Trent, the last example of this cottage industry, closed on 25 March 2012 when the end of terrace house they were served from was scheduled for demolition. More than 5,000 people signed a petition to save the oatcake shop, which had existed for more than 100 years. The popularity of oatcakes lives on, however, and the inaugural Oatcake Day took place on 8 August 2010, although some in north Staffordshire will tell you every day is oatcake day.

Branston Pickle

Named after the village of Branston, near Burton upon Trent, where the pickle was first produced in 1922 by Crosse and Blackwell, the brand is now owned by Burntwood-based food firm Mizkan. The Crosse and Blackwell food preserving plant in Branston was acquired from the government and had originally been commissioned as the National Machine Gun Factory. The brick wall at the front of the factory was built by German prisoners of war. As the building wasn't completed until the end of the First World War, no guns were ever produced there. Two thirds of the staff were women and Branston Lodge on the Burton Road was used as a residence for single female employees. Due to financial pressures, production was moved to London and the Branston factory was closed in January 1925. A fire in 2004 destroyed the former factory building.

Adams Dairies

In 1922, Fred Adams and his son, also Fred, began producing butter at a small dairy farm on the Buxton Road, the first in the country to produce pre-packed butter. By 1975, Adams Dairies was known as Adams Food Ltd, and was the largest butter-selling organisation in the country. The company was bought out by the Irish Dairy Board and in 1989 it was taken over by Kerrygold, who based their headquarters in Leek.

Yeomanry Pudding

A jam and egg custard tart dating back to the Boer War known as Staffordshire Yeomanry Pudding was first baked to celebrate the homecoming of men in the Staffordshire Yeomanry, a division of the Queen's Own Regiment and was a speciality at the Swan Hotel in Lichfield.

Elkes Biscuits

Malted milk biscuits were first produced by Elkes Biscuits in Uttoxeter in 1924. Elkes celebrated its 75th anniversary in 2003, and the business was first established in 1908, when Charles Henry Elkes opened a teashop on Carter Street in Uttoxeter. The company merged with Fox's Biscuits in 2004.

GRAPE AND GRAIN

According to Samuel Johnson, 'There is nothing which has yet been contrived by man, by which so much happiness is produced as by a good tavern or inn', and many of our Staffordshire pubs serve up tales alongside their ales.

Pubs and Inns

The **Bowling Green** pub in Lichfield has existed since the seventeenth century, as has the bowling green, which it is named after. For a while it was the residence of a hermit known as John Edwards. According to his obituary in the *Lichfield Mercury*:

> he came to the neighbourhood in the prime of life but behaved as a perfect stranger, retiring with disgust or disappointment from other and brighter scenes of life. The subscriptions of the

benevolent have contributed to shed a comparative comfort on his latter days and the medical gentlemen gratuitously attended him during his illness. A short time previous to his decease, he published a short 'Essay on Freemasonry'.

The **Goats Head** at Abbots Bromley has a room named after Dick Turpin, to commemorate the night he spent there after supposedly stealing Black Bess from Rugeley Horse Fair. One of his favourite establishments was reportedly the now closed Coach and Horses in Lichfield, kept by Judith Jackson, a famous beauty and a powerful, unscrupulous woman, making her an efficient ally of Turpin and his men.

The **Sheet Anchor** at Baldwin's Gate is the only pub of that name in the country and refers to a large, strong anchor used in an emergency.

There was a pub in the village of Pipe Ridware until 1919 when its license wasn't renewed after one of the punters threw a tankard at the bells of the nearby church during a service.

The **Four Crosses** at Cannock was a well-known coaching inn on Watling Street, owned by the Hatherton Family until the 1950s when it was sold to Bank's Brewery. It was managed by members of the Lovatt family for around 200 years until the death of Miss Lovatt in 1940 at the age of 91. At the time she was said to be the country's oldest licensee. The timber-framed section of the building dates back to 1636 – the date is carved into one of the exterior wooden beams – and the red brick extension dates to around 1700. When Miss Lovatt's great nephew, Harry Tomlison, was running the pub an old coachman's uniform, consisting of a velvet top and pair of buckskin trousers and dating to the 1820s, was discovered. According to local folklore it was found up a chimney but records held at the County Museum at Shugborough show the uniform was found in a trunk in an attic by Tomlinson's daughter Mary.

The **Star Inn** at Burntwood is where local nailers would take their products to be weighed and paid for by the middlemen who would also replenish their supplies of iron.

Ye Olde Windmill at Gentleshaw takes its name from 'ye olde windmill' in its beer garden.

The Leopard in Burslem dates to the early 1700s and was the setting for the first meeting between Josiah Wedgewood and James Brindley to discuss the creation of the Trent and Mersey Canal. In 1850, Charles Darwin lent his cook Mart and his butler Pepper Lees the money to buy the pub. In 1878, ambitious plans saw the pub extended in an attempt to create 'The Savoy of the North' and fifty-seven bedrooms were added to the existing Georgian ones. However, these were sealed off in the 1950s.

The Cross Keys in Hednesford was built in 1746 and is one of the oldest buildings in the town, originally a staging post for coaches and road wagons. Between 1904 and 1994, Hednesford Football Club played on a patch of land behind the pub and, although the ground is now a housing estate, the pub retains strong links with the club.

The **Yew Tree** at Cauldon Low is well known for its collection of antiques and curiosities, including Queen Victoria's stockings, a 3,000-year-old Grecian urn, penny farthings and a musical instrument known as the Serpent, all of which can be enjoyed along with a range of local ales from the comfort of the pub's antique chairs and benches.

The **King's Head** at Lichfield is thought to be the oldest pub in the city, dating back to 1408. It was one of the city's many coaching inns but is best known for being the home of the Staffordshire Regiment. In March 1705, Colonel Luke Lilingston raised a regiment of foot at the inn, later to become the 1st Staffordshire Regiment, as recorded on a bronze plaque on the outside wall of the pub.

The **Black Lion Inn** at Consall once served workers in the limestone industry in the Churnet Valley and there are four limekilns near to the pub.

The **Moorland Inn** in Burslem was once owned by darts player Eric Bristow, during which time it was known as 'The Crafty Cockney'.

The **Old Stone Cross** in Tamworth is the town's oldest pub and takes its name from the cross in the town's market place, where butchers sharpened their knives. The pub was visited by the Rolling Stones after they played at the Tamworth Assembly Rooms in December 1963, and Mick Jagger was reputedly barred for urinating up against the bar.

The **Three Tuns** in Lichfield, now recently reopened as The Barn, was taken over by F.H. Shilcock in September 1938 and he remained there for fifteen years. Mr Shilcock was also a poet and in 1950 a collection of his work, *Poems by a Lichfield Innkeeper*, was published.

Many Staffordshire pubs have been lost but perhaps none so literally as the **White Lion** of Stafford. The timber-framed building was taken down to make way for a ring road in the 1970s, with the intention it would be reconstructed elsewhere in the town. The pub's bricks, timber fixture, fittings and all, were put into storage but unfortunately no one could remember exaclty where, and despite an appeal from a Staffordshire county councillor in 2004, Stafford's White Lion remains at large.

The **Linford Arms** is one of the oldest buildings in Cannock and is where Charles Linford ran his carpentry firm from, later expanding his business to include an ironmongers, glaziers and sawmill.

With its own malthouse and brewery onsite, the **Bird and Hand Inn** at Hilderstone was one of the last remaining pubs in the county to brew its own beer. Brewing ceased in 1927 and the inn closed in 2005.

Breweries
In 1902, Burton upon Trent was described as, 'One vast brewery, a very city of beer … a beeropolis'. At one time, Burton upon Trent accounted for a quarter of all beer production in the UK and a technique in brewing known as Burtonisation is the act of adding sulphate to water, to emulate the chemical composition of the water in the town.

A brewery in Great Haywood obtained water using a steam engine. When water was extracted from the on-site well, all of the other wells in the village dried up.

Joule's Brewery was established in Stone in 1780 by Francis Joule at a site alongside the Trent and Mersey Canal. The town had a long history of brewing dating back to the twelfth century and the monks at Stone Priory. The new brewery continued the monks' tradition of marking their barrels with the sign of the cross and this became the registered trademark of the brewery, the sixth oldest beer mark in the world. The company exported its ale all over the world and was the first English brewer to supply bars in New York. Joule's was taken over by Bass Charrington and closed in 1972. The brewery was demolished, although a warehouse building alongside the canal still stands. A new brewery was established in Market Drayton in 2010, using the Joule's brand, methods and brewing notes and Joule's Pale Ale went back on sale at midday on 25 October of that year, exactly thirty-six years to the day that the last Joule's beer was brewed.

During an initiation ceremony at Joule's Brewery, known as 'trussing the cooper', a newly qualified cooper would be placed into a barrel he had made, and a mixture of soot, feathers, treacle and of course beer would be added. The barrel was rolled around the yard and the cooper was then taken out and tossed in the air three times.

Bass Brewery was founded in 1777 in Burton upon Trent; its main brand was Bass Pale Ale, once the best selling beer in the UK. The famous red triangle became the first brand to be registered under the UK's Trademark Registration Act of 1875 after an employee spent New Year's Eve queuing outside the registrar's office. Their red diamond became the country's second registered trademark.

Worthington's Brewery, founded in Burton in 1761, is the second oldest continuously brewed beer brand in the country after Whitbread.

In 1900, in many towns and cities across the north and west of the country, there was a huge rise in cases of what was originally thought to be alcohol-related neuritis. Eventually doctors in Manchester, one of the worst hit places, began to suspect that alcohol may not be the cause. After discovering arsenic in samples of local beer their suspicions were confirmed, and it was discovered that people were in fact being poisoned. There were thought to be around 6,000 cases of poisoning across the country, of which at least seventy were fatal. On 15 February 1901, the *Mercury* reported that ninety-one cases were discovered in the Lichfield urban district but there were no fatalities. All of these were traced back to the **Lichfield Brewery Company**.

The Titanic Brewery was founded in Burslem, Stoke-on-Trent, in 1985, its name a nod to the fact that Captain Smith of the ill-fated ship was born down the road in Hanley. The theme is also reflected in the range of beers: Steerage, Iceberg, Whitestar, Lifeboat and First Class. In 1996, the company also started brewing at the Shugborough estate in a log-fired Victorian brewery.

Slater's Ales, formerly the Eccleshall Brewery, was established behind the George Hotel in 1995, in the same location as the original brewery. In 2004, the business moved to new premises in Stafford and, in 2016, opened its first pub in the centre of Wolverhampton.

Lymestone Brewery in Stone brews a range of ales, each one named along the same theme, including Stone the Crows, Stone Faced, Foundation Stone and Ein Stein. The brewery operates from the former Bents Brewery site where there is a beehive on the roof, producing honey for the Stone Brood ale.

Freedom Brewery is the longest established craft lager brewer in Britain, opening in London in 1995 but relocating to Abbots Bromley in 2004.

Quartz in King's Bromley is an independent, family owned microbrewery founded in 2005.

Burton Bridge Brewery, built in the seventeenth century as the Fox and Goose Inn, takes its name from the bridge over the River Trent. Although situated 20 yards away from the present bridge, the old bridge came up to the front door.

Brewing at **Blythe Bridge** in Hamstall Ridware began in 2003, with two beers. Five regular beers are now produced alongside seasonal and speciality beers, with all ales named after local people, places and events: including Johnson's, Staffie, Palmer's Poison, Chase Bitter and Ridware Pale.

Wincle Brewery is over the border in Cheshire but brews beer with a Staffordshire flavour including the Wibbly Wallaby, referring to the marsupials still believed to inhabit the Roaches, after being set free from a private zoo. Sir Philip and Burke's Special are named after the squire of Swythalmley Hall and his faithful companion.

The **Peakstones Rock Brewery** produced its first batch of beer in May 2005, an amber bitter named after the Nemisis ride at the nearby Alton Towers theme park. Nine ales are now produced at the plant in the Staffordshire Moorlands, continuing the theme park theme with Oblivion and Black Hole but also taking names inspired by the surrounding landscape and its stories. Pugin's Gold was brewed to celebrate the 200th birthday of Augustus Pugin, architect of St Giles Roman Catholic Church in Cheadle, and the brewery opened its first micropub and microbrewery in the Moorlands, at Blythe Bridge, in July 2015.

The **Langot Valley vineyard** is 5 miles from the market town of Eccleshall, and its name comes from the French word meaning tongue shaped, which may have been introduced by French glassworkers in the area in the sixteenth century. The sandy soil, which attracted them to the area, is also perfect for growing vines.

Buzzards Valley is a family run vineyard near Tamworth where 8,000 vines are grown over 7 acres.

In 1983, the first half-acre of vines was planted at **Halfpenny Green Vineyards,** and today there are almost 30 acres. A winery was added in 2005, producing around 50 to 60,000 bottles of wine of Halfpenny Green wine each year.

7

STAFFORDSHIRE ARCHITECTURE

STATUES AND SCULPTURE

The sailor guarding the entrance to Lichfield Registry Office (once the Free Library and Museum) was originally created for the War Memorial in Duncombe Place by York, but after it was rejected on the basis it was too warlike it was given to the city by the stonemason and architect Robert Bridgeman.

Until recently, a bronze sculpture of a stag and hind stood in High Green Court shopping centre in Cannock. The sculpture was won by a local woman who won it on the game show *The Price is Right* and donated it to the town as a gift.

There is a sculpture of a Marmite jar next to the library in Burton upon Trent, nicknamed Monumite.

A statue of Samuel Johnson sits in the Market Square in Lichfield, opposite his former home, now the Samuel Johnson Birthplace Museum. Each year, the city celebrates the birthday of one of its most famous sons, and a wreath is laid on the statue by the Mayor of Lichfield.

A wooden statue dedicated to the memory of Christina Collins, murdered whilst travelling by narrowboat along the Trent and Mersey Canal in June 1839, stands below the Workhouse Bridge in Stone. Christina raised her fears about the intentions of the men she was travelling with to Hugh Cordwell at the Toll Office here but he did nothing but advise her to report the crew at the end of her journey. Christina's body was found in the canal at Rugeley the following day.

A statue of Captain John Smith of the *Titanic* stands in Lichfield's Beacon Park. On several occasions the people of Hanley have requested that the statue be returned to them, on the basis that Smith was born there and that the statue was originally intended for the town but rejected due to the perceived shame associated with the sinking of the ship. However, the bronze sculpture, created by Kathleen Scott, widow of Scott of the Antarctic, was never intended for Hanley. It was erected in Lichfield, as it was the centre of the diocese and was also a convenient place for people travelling between London and Liverpool to visit. Ironically, it was actually in Lichfield where opposition to the statue was greatest. A petition was presented to the City Council protesting that Smith has no connection with Lichfield and therefore a statue was inappropriate. In 2012, a memorial service was held at the statue with 1,523 tea lights placed at the foot of the statue to remember those who lost their lives in the disaster.

The place name Shenstone is thought to mean 'shining stone', a fact which inspired Jo Naden's steel sculpture for the village's Lammas Land in 2002. The silver stone sculpture was placed at a point where a bridge crosses the Black Brook stream running through the Lammas Lands. Trees can be seen reflected in the stainless steel, and the text inscribed on it – 'A flock of birds settle ... the green field re-echoes where there is a brisk bright stream' – is taken from the words of an unknown ninth-century Irish author.

Fifteen pigs decorated by local school, businesses and organisations as part of the I Am Tamworth project in 2015 were intended to be a temporary public art display but proved so popular that they are now a permanent fixture in the town.

Each of the fifteen pigs represents an aspect of the town's identity and history: Hogred the Boar in the castle grounds, the King of Merskia painted in the colours of the Mercian flag and located near to the Snowdome, and Bobby the Peeler, decorated by the Peel Society and located next to the statue of the former prime minister and police founder in Marker Street.

A Sheela-na-gig was discovered at Alstonefield by an amateur archaeologist examining a pile of old stones. The Romanesque sculpture depicts a monster eating a woman exposing herself and may have been created as a warning against lust.

Khushi the elephant in Cannock town centre is a replacement for the vandalised Canumbo, aka Nocky, a fibreglass model of an elephant commissioned by WHSmith Do it All in 1989. No one seems to know why Canumbo existed in the first place although it has been suggested it may have been a reference to the private zoo kept by Dr John Kerr Butter at his home on the Wolverhampton Road. As well as an elephant, Butter also kept giraffes, ostriches and chimpanzees and other exotic animals, and visited patients in a zebra-drawn carriage.

A cow on a flying carpet was one of around twenty or so sculptures created for an arts project between Stafford Borough Council and Stafford College. Some of the artworks were vandalised and it was reported that the model of a giant shark, which was part of the sculpture trail, was tipped into the River Sow.

Keele's Dragon is made of bronze and has removable wings and is thought to be one of a pair of giant boot-scrapers, originally made for Keele Hall at Gresham's Apedale Works in the early twentieth century. It was discovered in three pieces on a rubbish dump in 1951 by Dr Ron Evans who repaired it and called it Herbert. Herbert lived outside the Evans' home in Keele village but was frequently dragon-napped. Some of his adventures

have caused him to end up on a bonfire, be painted bright blue and to be introduced to HRH Princess Margaret. In 2006, Mairwen Evans and her daughter Catryn presented Herbert to the university in Ron's memory, and since 2010 he has resided in the atrium of the university library.

Two prime ministers are commemorated in the grounds of Sandon Hall. A Doric column erected in 1806 marks the death of William Pitt the Younger, a close friend of the first Earl of Harrowby who had acted as his second in a duel on Putney Heath in 1798. The pistols used by Pitt in the duel were given to the Earl and are on display at Sandon Hall. A shrine on the hillside in Sandon Park is dedicated to the assassinated Prime Minister Spencer Perceval, also a close friend of the Earl.

The eighteenth-century Shepherds' Monument in the grounds of Shugborough Hall contains a code that intellectuals such as Charles Darwin, Charles Dickens and former codebreakers from Bletchley Park have tried, but failed, to crack. Below a mirror image of Nicolas Poussin's 'Shepherds of Arcadia' there is a sequence of letters, O U O S V A V V, between the letters D and M. Interpretations have ranged from a secret love message to instructions on how to find the Holy Grail, but the monument refuses to give ups its secret easily.

The statue of a lion outside the Council Offices in Leek was originally commissioned for Alton Towers by the 15th Earl of Shrewsbury in the 1820s and was donated to the town by a benefactor in 1924.

A statue of Robert Peel, his head turned towards his home at Drayton Manor, stands in front of the Town Hall in Tamworth, close to where the former prime minister and founder of the Metropolitan Police Force delivered his Tamworth Manifesto to the electors of Tamworth in December 1834.

BRICKS AND STONES

Outside the entrance to the church at Grindon is a 'rindle stone', erected by the Lord of the Manor to record that he had established his right to the rindle, a small brook which only runs in wet weather, at Stafford Assizes on 17 March 1872.

A stone with markings resembling a cross in a circle was found being used as a stone trough in a field in Cresswell and was possibly thought to be a relic from a private chapel at the now ruined Paynsley Hall. The stone was mounted in the grounds of St Mary's Catholic Church in the village where it was spotted by a historian who identified the mysterious stone as part of an old cheese press.

The Herringbone Wall at Tamworth Castle dates back to around AD 1180 and is considered one of the finest examples of Norman masonry of this kind in the country.

The Jubilee Stone at Rudyard Lake commemorates Queen Victoria's Diamond Jubilee in 1897. The stone came from a local quarry and while transporting it from there to its current position it was broken. A small joint is visible where it was cemented together.

An ancient boundary stone, which marked the limits of the Cathedral Close and was visited by choristers as part of the Beating the Bounds ceremony on Ascension Day, can be found incorporated in the right-hand gatepost of the Garden of Remembrance in Lichfield.

The origins of a tiled wall plaque set into the brickwork of a property on Market Street, Hednesford, which has the motto of the Order of the Garter and the Royal Standard of Queen Victoria, are unknown but it has been suggested that the panel may commemorate a royal coronation.

A 'bishop's heap of stones' was once found between Canwell Hall and Hints, and there are at least two possible explanations for why a pile of pebbles was associated with a bishop. The more fanciful of the two suggests that they were placed there in memory of a bishop and his attendants who were robbed and murdered as they travelled along the road there. However, a more likely reason, given in the seventeenth century by a centenarian known as Bess of Blackbrook, is that when visiting his home town of Sutton Coldfield, John Vesey, the Bishop of Exeter between 1518 and 1554, was annoyed by the rolling pebbles on the road which caused travellers' horses to stumble and sometimes fall and so he employed poor people to gather them up into heaps.

In 1949, the central spire of Lichfield Cathedral was found to be in such a poor state that more than twenty-two of the stone courses had to be removed and redressed or replaced, work which was funded by the public via the Lichfield Spire Repair Fund. The architect on the job, George Pace, later stated that the spire had been at risk of falling through the roof of the cathedral. Interestingly, on removing the gilded ball from the spire, it was found to contain several rolls of parchment, a half-ounce of twist and the remains of half a pint of beer!

A row of nineteenth-century terrace houses in Sherburne Road in Stoke has a line of tiles, each with the word 'Gold Coin' running below the upper windows. Reputedly, the man who built the houses did so with the money won by betting on a horse called Gold Coin and put a gold sovereign behind one of the tiles on each house for good luck.

The orangery at Woodhouse Farm, formerly part of the Fisherwick estate owned by Lord Donegall and designed by Capability Brown, and subsequently used as a mushroom house and cow shed, was scheduled for demolition in the 1970s after it was struck by lightning. However, it escaped demolition and still remains today, a fitting reminder of the former glory of the estate and its subsequent fall.

Thomas Spencer, co-founder of Marks and Spencer, came to live in Whittington to pursue his love of farming after retiring from the partnership, which began on 28 September 1894 when he invested £300 into a business owned by Michael Marks. The church hall is named after him, built with funding from the retailer in 1984.

The Holy Austin Rock Houses at Kinver Edge were the last troglodyte homes to be occupied in England and have been restored by the National Trust to reflect the lives of their former inhabitants. One of the rock houses was a hermitage until the Reformation.

The Lady of the Lake is the oldest of the boathouses at Rudyard Lake and is named after the ship's figurehead, which is incorporated into the chimney. Another ship's figurehead was placed at the entrance to Lud's Church in around 1862 by the landowner, Philip Brocklehurst of Swythamley. It was intended to commemorate the supposed martyrdom of the daughter of a Lollard preacher, and remained there until the early twentieth century.

The Shepherd's Cross at Biddulph is a fourteenth-century stone carved from millstone grit. Its purpose is unknown although it has been described as a wayside marker.

The Red Cross at St John's Church in Knypersley is another possible wayside marker, moved here in 1943 from the crossroads near Knypersely Hall, via Red Cross Hall.

BRIDGES

The Georgian bridge over the moat at Sinai Park was built in 1732 and is thought to have replaced a timber bridge, where it's said a skirmish between the Pagets and the Bagots of Blithfield took place during the Civil War, leaving musket balls lodged in some of the house's beams.

The Hanging Bridge, spanning the River Dove, and also the Staffordshire/Derbyshire boundary, was rebuilt in 1937 but the arches of the original fourteenth-century packhorse bridge are still visible. The name is said to refer to the executions of the Jacobite rebels, which took place here although etymology suggests otherwise.

The Marmion Stone near to the entrance of Tamworth Castle is more commonly known as the Wishing Chair. It originated as a pedestal supporting a figure of St Mary on the medieval Lady Bridge, which was destroyed in a flood in 1795 and was placed in the wall of the replacement bridge until it was moved to its present location in 1872. The stone marked the boundary of land owned by the Marmions of the castle from that of the land owned by the Bassett family of Drayton Manor and featured the coats of arms of both families, although these have been all but worn away by the ravages of time and weather.

The Ferry Bridge in Burton upon Trent replaced the ferryboat, which once operated across the River Trent, and was a gift to the town from Michael Arthur Bass in 1889. Baron Burton also paid off the town corporation's loan for purchasing the ferry rights from the Marquis of Anglesey meaning that Burtonians no longer needed to pay a toll to cross the bridge. In 1771, the ferry keeper's cottage was replaced by the Ferry House, which also functioned as a public house until 1825. Its licence was revoked in 1825 after a local baronet trying to cross the river was ignored by the ferry keeper who was otherwise engaged in his other role as publican; the baronet was forced to wade across the river.

Cherry Eye Bridge, over the Caldon Canal near Froghall, is said to take its name from the red, inflamed eyes of the miners who crossed it on their way to and from the nearby ironstone mine.

In 1815, the postman who was usually responsible for taking mail to the villages of the Ridwares fell ill, and so the task fell to his colleague, 21-year-old James Pinson. Despite being an inexperienced horseman, James was given a blind pony to carry out the job. As darkness fell and they crossed the old and narrow Colton Mill Bridge near Rugeley, something spooked the sightless mount, who vaulted over the low parapet of the bridge, landing in the field below. The pony was killed instantly but Pinson was unharmed. Until the bridge was replaced in 1890, there was a crude inscription recording the accident for posterity (or perhaps mischief), which read, 'J. Pinson's Leap 1816'. Over the years the story became embellished to the extent that someone wrote to the *Staffordshire Advertiser* asking that Pinson's bravery in jumping his horse into the river rather than surrendering the mail he was carrying to a gang of ruffians should be marked by a plaque on the new bridge.

The Essex Bridge over the River Trent, on the edge of the Shugborough estate near Great Haywood, is rumoured to have been built by the second Earl of Essex to allow Elizabeth I to visit him at Chartley Castle. It is the least altered bridge in the country and the longest remaining packhorse bridge in England with fourteen of its original forty-three arches surviving.

High Bridge crosses the River Trent and in July 1403 was the meeting place of two feuding neighbours, both en route to fight on opposite sides at the Battle of Shrewsbury. Sir William Handsacre was for the rebel Sir Henry 'Hotspur' Percy and Sir Robert Mavesyn was loyal to the king. Mavesyn killed Handsacre but met his own end shortly afterwards – 'standing with the king and fighting by his side even unto death', according to the epitaph on his tombstone at the church of St Nicholas at Mavesyn Ridware.

MAKING YOUR MARK

Some tiles at the site of Letocetum at Wall near Lichfield are marked with the initials and sometimes the fingerprints of the workmen who made them. A cat's paw print can also be seen on one of the tiles.

The 'Bride's Hand' is the outline of a female hand carved into the stonework of the south porch of St James the Great at Longdon. It's an old tradition that brides arriving at the church would place their own hand against it, in the hope that it would bring good fortune and fertility to their impending marriage – a tradition still carried on by Longdon brides-to-be.

During restoration work on the tower of St Peter's, Alstonefield, a series of outlines of shoes and hands, with dates from the eighteenth and nineteenth centuries, were discovered carved into the lead of the roof, together with the outline of a clock face.

The names of former pupils of Lichfield Grammar School can be found carved into the stone and woodwork of the building, now used as the Lichfield District Council Offices, including in the attics, once used as dormitories by boarders at the school.

One of the most intriguing features at the church of St Lawrence in Gnosall can be found high on the south side of the church where stonemasons who extended the tower in the mid fifteenth century have carved a large chalice into the stonework alongside the belfry window.

Mary, Queen of Scots is believed to have stayed overnight at Abbots Bromley's Manor House during what was to be her last journey. A pane of glass with the inscription *Maria Regina Scotiae quondam transibat istam villam 21 Septembris 1585 usque Burton*, said to have been scratched by Mary with a diamond ring, was taken from the house and is now in the William Salt Library.

When the owners of the fourteenth-century Pear Tree Cottage in Yoxall stripped away paint from the walls of the hall in 2004, they discovered a series of medieval inscriptions etched into the wall. These included drawings of heads, birds, interlocking circles thought to be apotropaic and the figure of a knight with a banner. There were also the place names 'Bromley' and 'Yoxall', spelt three different ways.

It's rumoured that the cellar beneath the Tudor Cafe on Bore Street was used as a prison during the Civil War, and graffiti there carved into an old oak door includes, *Cave adsum* and 'God with us', both mottos of the parliamentarians, together with a crude carving of a hanged man, with the name Hampden alongside.

A pair of gate pillars from the demolished Fisherwick Hall, displaying two carved coronets, amidst 200 years worth of graffiti, including a 'lucky' horseshoe, have been reassembled on Fisherwick Green.

At the Four Crosses Inn near Cannock, a verse attributed to Sir Thomas More, which reads, *Fleres si scires unum tua tempora mensem. Rides cum non sit forsitan una dies*, is carved onto one of the external beams above a ground-floor window.

The town ditch surrounding Lichfield was about 5m wide and 2m deep in the St John's Street area. Inevitably, it was also used as a public tip and archaeologists examining a section in the car park of the Lichfield District Council Offices recovered a twelfth-century woman's shoe, part of a medieval jug and the remains of a medieval dog's head.

STAIRWAYS

An Australian couple, Bill and Ursula Hayward, honeymooning in Britain, acquired some of the oak panelling, doors and windows along with the grand 'Waterloo Staircase' from Beaudesert Hall, all of which they incorporated in Carrick House, their English manor-style home in Adelaide. Carrick House is now used as a public museum and art gallery.

The rare double spiral staircase at St Editha's Church allows two people to climb the tower at the same time without seeing each other until they reach the top.

At Brindley Bank, near Rugeley, a set of steps leading up from the canal are known as 'The Bloody Steps', after Christina Collins' body was carried up them to the Talbot Inn, her body having been found in the canal here. Local folklore suggests that blood is sometimes seen oozing from the steps and that Christina's ghost has been witnessed here too.

It's said that no one going up or down the Devil's Staircase in Consall ever counts the same number of steps twice.

In 1949, a prize was offered by Mr J.W. Horwood of BW Investigations to produce evidence that ghosts do exist. The editor of the Birmingham magazine *Home News* accepted the challenge, and spent a night at Tamworth Castle in the hope that he would capture the spectre of a nun said to walk the staircase after midnight. As the clock struck, the air on the staircase turned cold and Horwood heard footsteps on the wood of the stairs. Horwood took a photo which when developed showed a shadowy figure descending the stairs. Whether Horwood accepted this as evidence is unknown.

Crakemarsh Hall was rebuilt in 1815, around a seventeenth-century carved oak staircase salvaged from the former hall. When the hall was demolished, the staircase was saved once again and was on sale in late 2015 for a price of £64,000.

8

NATURAL STAFFORDSHIRE

NATURAL PHENOMENA

During the fourteenth century, a monk called William de Schepisheved recorded events in the annals of Croxden Abbey including a great earthquake which took place, with all the persons in the convent 'being at their first refection, were dismayed with a sudden and unlooked-for trembling'. An eclipse of the sun was recorded on 9 July 1330 and this was seen as a portent of bad weather to come. It was recorded that great floods of rainwater spread and the harvest was not able to ripen, with many places in the country unable to gather in crops until Michaelmas that year.

According to Robert Plot, on 4 November 1678 a dreadful earthquake at Brewood came with a rumbling noise like thunder, so great that it awakened people in their beds and continued until two o'clock in the morning.

In November 1795, Tamworth was hit by an earthquake that cracked the masonry of the Lady Bridge.

Each summer solstice, the sun sets twice in Leek. Traditionally, the double sunset was viewed from the area of the churchyard at St Edward's known as the Doctors' Corner. However, it is alleged that trees planted in the 1960s to deliberately obscure the view due to its pagan connotations prevent the phenomenon being seen from the churchyard, although it can still be witnessed from other parts of the town.

In September 1708, heavy rain caused a considerable amount of damage in Rugeley, destroying a stone bridge and running along the streets of the town with such force that it made several holes and undermined several houses.

In January 1852, a farmer called John Plant from Leekfrith recorded in his diary that he had lost his ferret whilst out catching rabbits in a thunderstorm.

In the parish register of Wombourne Church it is recorded that a storm at Trysull on 25 May 1640 split an elm tree and caused stones to be struck out of the church wall, leading people to believe that the church had been on fire.

GEOLOGICAL FEATURES

The Winking Man pub near Leek takes its name from a rock formation at Ramshaws Rocks, where a face seems to wink at you as you drive uphill to the pub.

The Geohut at Alstonefield contains an exhibition of the local geology, featuring a variety of rock samples from the surrounding area.

Several of the rock formations at Dovedale have been given names, including Lovers' Leap, the Twelve Apostles, Lion's Head Rock and Tissington Spires.

Beeston Tor is a limestone cliff overlooking the confluence of the River Hamps and the River Manifold. Until 1934, there was a station here, part of the Leek and Manifold narrow-gauge railway.

On 14 September 1926, Ralph de Tunstall Sneyd, Chief Bard of the Order of the Imperishable Sacred Land, held a gorsedd of druids, bards and ovates ceremony at Thor's Cave, located in a limestone crag above the River Manifold. Over 2,000 people came to witness the procession along the path between Wetton and the cave where the ceremony was conducted in both English and Welsh. The following year, the second and final gorsedd was held at the cave with a more select audience of 100 ticket holders. The cave was used as a location for the 1988 Ken Russell film *The Lair of the White Worm*. Below Thor's Cave is a second cavern known as Thor's Fissure Cavern, which is also known as 'Radcliffe's Stable' after a man who is said to have concealed his horse there from the Scottish rebel army in 1745.

Lud's Church is a natural chasm above Gradbach, in an area known as the Black Forest. This cleft in the millstone grit was formed by a landslip and is the setting for several local legends, supposedly providing a hiding place for Robin Hood and Bonny Prince Charlie as well as a secret place of worship for the Lollards in the fifteenth century.

Charles Darwin identified a geological fault in Butterton, created by an upthrust of volcanic lava, and it was nicknamed 'Darwin's Dyke' in his honour. A piece of rock from the dyke was donated to the MIR space station by Phil Parker and signed by all three cosmonauts on board.

TREES AND PLANTS

Erasmus Darwin, one of only three members of the Lichfield Botanic Society alongside Sir Brook Boothby and John Jackson, created a botanic garden around a mile from his home on Beacon Street, Lichfield, on the site where physician Dr John Floyer had previously established a cold bath fed by a spring known as Unett's Well. The garden was described by Anna Seward as 'a little, wild umbrageous valley' and was restored by the Worthington family of Maples Hayes in the late nineteenth century.

The feast day of St Chad, the first Bishop of Lichfield, which falls on 2 March, is said to be the most propitious day of the year for sowing broad beans.

A Gospel Tree marked on OS maps of Gentleshaw up until the 1930s was a parish boundary marker. When perambulating the boundary at certain times of the year, the villagers would have stopped to say prayers and hear passages read from the Bible.

When the Cherry Wakes were held at the Three Tuns Inn in Lichfield, crowds of visitors would arrive to enjoy the ripe white heart cherries grown in an adjoining orchard, and wash them down with ale. Another area of the city is still known as Cherry Orchard and fruit trees can still be found growing in amongst the houses.

In years gone by, the fruit of the damson trees growing in the hedgerows of Bishop's Wood was sent to Liverpool where it was used to dye naval uniforms, with the leftover pulp being utilised by the jam factories.

The current Cank Thorn, opposite the Commonwealth War Cemetery, is planted on the site of the original tree at the meeting point of three ancient manor boundaries. It is believed the tree is not found growing anywhere else in the wild and is therefore unique to Cannock Chase.

Cannock Chase has its own fruit, the Cannock Chase Bilberry, a rare hybrid between a bilberry and a cowberry.

Between 1860 and 1901, Stone hosted the All England Gooseberry Growing Competition. For over 100 years, a gooseberry grown in the town by John Flower and weighing thirty-seven pennyweights and seven grains held the record as the world's biggest.

The John Downie is considered one of the finest of all the crab apples and it was first raised by Mr R. Holmes at Whittington in 1875 who named it after his friend and fellow nurseryman. The 'rich orange red fruits' are ripe in October and a tree can be found outside the hall in the village.

The Elford Pippin raised by Mr Darlaston in the village between Lichfield and Tamworth was an excellent dessert apple with yellow, tender crisp flesh and a fine, brisk sugary and vinous flavour.

Prince's Park in Burntwood contains three trees named Faith, Hope and Charity. The park, created to commemorate the marriage of Albert, Prince of Wales to Princess Alexandra of Denmark, is included in the *Guinness Book of Records* as the smallest park in the United Kingdom and the World's Shortest Fun Run took place there in both 2013 and 2016.

At Beaudesert Park, there was a hollow oak tree, which could accommodate eight people. A hole in the trunk was used by Lady Uxbridge to place a telescope in, enabling her to observe objects in the surrounding countryside. Another tree in the park, the Roan Oak, has branches that have twisted into shapes resembling a writhing serpent and a crouching lion and there is also said to be a magic oak, haunted by evil spirits.

A medieval holly hedge at Keele University is listed as an ancient monument.

Wheaton Aston is the most northerly point in the UK where snake's head fritillary has been found growing wild and the flower is used as the village's unofficial emblem.

The Beggars Oak in Bagot's Park in the Needwood Forest is believed to have been given its name as any traveller had the right to a enjoy a night's lodging beneath its branches.

Root House in Mayfield is a Gothic-style Georgian summerhouse created entirely from roots and branches.

With a circumference of 575ft (175m), a similar size to the auditorium at the Royal Albert Hall, the 350-year-old yew tree in the grounds of Shugborough Hall is officially the widest in Britain. The Tree Register of the British Isles lists it as the tree with the largest crown in Britain and Ireland, and it is suspected that it may even be the largest in Europe. Originally the yew had a tunnel running through it and it was used as a den by former residents of Shugborough Patrick Lichfield and his sister Elizabeth. In 2014, the tree was shortlisted as one of the Woodland Trust's top ten trees in Britain but the Shugborough Yew eventually lost out to Sherwood Forest's Major Oak.

A solitary tree, which once stood on top of High Shutt near Cheadle, was visible from miles around and according to legend it was used to execute highwaymen and other criminals. As a result, local folklore suggests the tree is cursed and that anyone walking around its trunk nine times will hear the sound of bells, summoning them to their death. The tree was also used as a meeting place for three young men who each went on to be a

Member of Parliament. Although the original tree died in the 1990s, another has since been planted on the site by the Cheadle Rotary Club.

The Chained Oak is part of a local legend which tells of a curse placed upon the Talbot family of Alton Towers, after the Earl of Shrewsbury turned away a beggar who asked him for a coin as he returned home one night. The curse stated that every time a branch fell from the oak tree one of the earl's family would die. That night, a storm caused a branch to fall from the tree and a member of the Talbot family died. Believing the curse to be true, the earl ordered the branched of the tree to be chained in an attempt to prevent further deaths. The legend inspired the Hex ride at Alton Towers theme park, and the tree with its chains can still be seen today. A significant part of the tree collapsed in April 2007 but it was confirmed that no members of the current earl's family had died suddenly or mysteriously as a result.

WATERS

At Newbold Manor, near Barton, several saline springs are said to have such an effect on the pastureland that it changes the colour of the cattle grazing there – from black, red or brown to a whitish dun.

It is said that rain running down the west side of Newpool Road in Biddulph and Knypersley will end up in the Irish Sea, whereas the gutters on the east side run to the North Sea.

In June 1858, a number of objects found in Stowe and Minster Pools in the City of Lichfield during their conversion into reservoirs for the South Staffordshire Waterworks Company, were presented to the Leicestershire Architectural and Archaeological Society. These included:

A small iron battle axe, seventeen inches in length, several narrow sharp pointed knives from 7 to 9 inches long of the sixteenth century, several keys of the fifteenth or sixteenth centuries and a small one of still older date, soles of shoes from the thirteenth, fourteenth and fifteenth centuries, a leaden seal or bull of one of the Popes whose name is obliterated and an angel of the seventeenth year of James I with a hole through it for suspension it having been given to a person when touched by the King for the evil. The reverse has a ship with the royal arms on the mainsail.

Another discovery in Minster Pool led to a court case in 1896 between South Staffordshire Waterworks Company and a labourer named Sharman. This case is still quoted as an example in legal textbooks today. Sharman, the defendant, had been employed by the water company to clean the pool and in the course of this work found two gold rings. The court ruled that it was not a matter of 'finders, keepers' and ordered the rings to be handed over.

Chartley Moss is one of England's largest floating bogs. A raft of peat up to 10ft thick floats on a 40ft-deep lake. Trees growing in the peat eventually sink under their own weight and drown as they mature, leaving dead trunks protruding. Due to the dangerous nature of the site, visits are only permitted when accompanied by a guide. The site is classified as a site of special scientific interest.

Sir William Wolseley lost his life on 8 July 1728 after visiting Lichfield in his coach and four. On his way there, he passed the Shropshire Brook, which runs across the road at Longdon, so shallow that it could easily be stepped over as the water was kept up by a milldam at some distance from the road. However, on his return journey, the milldam gave way and the water rushed across the road, overturning the carriage and drowning Sir William with his horses. The coachman was thrown off the box into a tree and escaped.

Rudyard Lake was constructed in 1799 to feed the Caldon Canal and soon became a tourist destination. It has its own navy with a frigate, battleship and hunter-killer submarine and the French acrobat, The Great Blondin, once walked across the lake on a tightrope. When the Horton Lodge boathouse on the edge of Rudyard Lake caught fire in February 1895, the fire brigade cut two holes in the frozen ice but were unable to save the building. Unable to winch the engine back onto the road due to the icy conditions, the engine was instead hauled across the lake by the fire crew and skaters. Later that month, the Leek Volunteers marched across the lake, playing songs, and all but the drummer and the sergeant instructor managed to keep their footing.

Betley Mere is one of the few natural standing waters in the county and was created by glacial drift.

WELLS

Writer, researcher and holy well expert Pixy Led has researched over forty holy wells in Staffordshire, the details of which are included on his blog insearchofholywellsandhealingsprings. wordpress.com. According to him, some of the county's most interesting sites are as follows:

The Egg Well at Bradnop, with its Latin inscription *Renibus, et spleni, cordi, jecorique medetur, Mille malis prodest ista salubris aqua*, which translates roughly as 'The kidneys, the spleen, the liver and the heart/ These waters cureth every part'. The name of the well may relate to the shape of the basin or possibly to the smell emitted by the sulphurous waters.

St John's Well at Shenstone is believed to be a place of healing and miracles at Midsummer.

The King's Well at Ellerton may take its name from local folklore that Charles I once stopped to take its waters although other sources suggest the name is a reference to his son who hid near to the well following the Battle of Worcester.

St Betram's Well in Ilam is named after the legendary Anglo-Saxon prince-turned-hermit, buried in the church. The well may be the stone structure built over a spring on Bunster Hill or the spring alongside the church.

Our Lady's Well in Wombourne is cut out of solid rock and was once home to a hermit. Its name derives from its dedication to the Virgin Mary in medieval times.

Nun's Well in Cannock Wood is a spring rising in a chamber cut from rock with a sixteenth-century Tudor-style brickwork arch. Legend has it that the well has healing powers, specifically for sore eyes, and takes its name from a nun who was murdered there. Centuries after she was pushed to her death, two farm labourers discovered her earthly remains in the sealed-up well and her ghost materialised before them.

St Helen's Well at Rushton Spencer, where there is a local belief that when the waters run dry, bad times will follow.

The Devil's Well at Betley, believed to be good for the eyes and is in fact dedicated to St Ottilia, a name which became corrupted to its current form over the centuries, although there is also a local legend that when the Devil was flying from Beeston Castle to Alsager a stone dropped out of his leather apron and the well sprang up where it hit the ground.

According to tradition, there was once a well in what is now Beacon Park in Lichfield known as **Maudlin's Well** after a drunkard tumbled in one evening on his way home from the pub.

At Stoneywell, between Lichfield and Rugeley, there was a round pool where a spring flowed from beneath a large boulder and it was believed locally that removing the stone would cause all the cattle in the surrounding area to be struck down with disease.

The Well in the Wall, between Upper and Lower Tean, arose from a large rock and was said to throw out small bones, like sparrows and chickens, all year round except for in July and August.

ANIMALS

Britain's first test-tube piglets were born at Teddesley Home Farm at Penkridge.

Molly Badham and Nathalie Evans were rival pet shop owners in Sutton Coldfield who joined forces to buy a three-quarter-acre plot in Hints Lane near Tamworth where they built a bungalow for both themselves and their menagerie of animals. Members of the public took great interest in the animals, including the chimps who went on to become famous for their TV advertising. The Hints Zoological Society opened its doors in 1954 and the collection of animals and the number of visitors grew to the point where a larger site was necessary, and in the summer of 1962 the society moved to the site at Twycross where it remains today. In 2003, Molly received an MBE for her contribution to the conservation of endangered species.

Legend has it that a Frenchman once took his dancing bear to be shod at the old blacksmiths on Beacon Street in Lichfield.

The Tamworth is thought to be the closest breed to what the old English forest pigs would have been like. It originated at Sir Robert Peel's Drayton Manor estate, after the existing herd was crossbred with Irish Grazing pigs in 1812. The most famous Tamworth Pigs were Butch and Sundance who on 8 January 1998 saved their own bacon by escaping from a lorry at an abattoir in Malmesbury, Wiltshire, and swimming across the

River Avon. After being on the run for a week, both pigs were taken to the Rare Breeds Centre in Woodchurch, Kent, where they lived out the rest of their days.

Purchaser and his fellow canine, Vendor, are buried in the grounds of a building in Lichfield that was once home to a firm of solicitors.

In 1946, two young men were spending a quiet Monday afternoon fishing at Stowe Pool in Lichfield when they noticed a cow swimming towards them. The heifer got out of the water, charged at them and then started swimming back towards Stowe Street. However, something must have changed its mind, as the cow then decided to turn around, charging at a policeman who had just arrived on the scene. By this time, the fishermen and the pool attendant were hiding behind Johnson's Willow. Deciding to make a run for it, the attendant headed for the boathouse and the two lads jumped over the hedge. Unfortunately, so did the cow. With the police officer in hot pursuit, the poor beast ran up The Windings and into a field, where finally, having calmed down, it stayed overnight before 'being removed' the following morning (the *Mercury* reporter thought it had been destroyed). Where the cow came from and what caused this odd behaviour is not known.

The churchyard at St Michael's in Lichfield was once let as pasture, although in 1801 the grazing of cattle was deemed inappropriate due to the 'damage and desecration' caused and it was decided that only sheep should be allowed. However, this was ignored with tragic consequences, as in 1809 there is an entry in the church register for the burial of a child, Joseph Harper, who was killed by a cow in the churchyard.

When the central spire of Lichfield Cathedral was restored following the Civil War, a live frog was said to have been found inside one of the stones.

Freda, a Harlequin Great Dane, was a mascot of the New Zealand Rifle Brigade who had been stationed at Brocton since September 1917. When Freda died in autumn 1918, she was buried on Cannock Chase and members of the brigade erected a headstone in her memory. After years of being tended to by the people of nearby Brereton, the grave was vandalised and the original headstone was replaced by the Friends of Cannock Chase in 1964. In 2010, a service for working dogs and their owners was held at the grave to celebrate the loyalty and service of these animals.

Since the late nineteenth century, the Staffordshire Regiment have had a mascot. Their first Staffordshire Bull Terrier, called Boxer, leapt from a train at Cairo and was presumed dead after being seen lying motionless at the side of the track. However, a few days later, the dog staggered into their camp and collapsed. Boxer had walked for 200 miles along the railway track to join his regiment. The current mascot, Watchman V, took over from the retired Watchman IV on 4 October 2009.

Legend has it that the last wolf to be killed in Staffordshire was slaughtered by Baron Brough of Brough Hall in Staffordshire, although another legend says that the Wolseley estate near Rugeley was granted to the family by King Edgar as a reward for ridding the area of wolves.

Basil the horse gained notoriety several years ago for regularly enjoying a pint of Pedigree at the bar of the Meynall Ingram Arms in the village of Hoar Cross.

A giant eel is said to have lived in a well behind Ye Olde Windmill Inn at Gentleshaw for many years.

A black panther, part of a menagerie kept by Sir John Giffard of Chillington Hall, escaped into the forest at Brewood. As the beast was about to attack a mother and child, Giffard shot it dead using a bow and arrow. As he did so his son shouted, 'Take breath, pull strong'. The site was marked with a wooden cross, which has been relocated in an attempt to conserve it. Giffard earned his family the crest of a panther's head and the Giffard family motto is the phrase used by his son.

The annual Fazeley Fair, which was held at the end of October in the nineteenth century, used to be one of the biggest events of its kind in the Midlands and would attract huge crowds. Monkeys, a dancing bear, tigers and lions were among the attractions and on one occasion, the landlord of the Town Hall Vaults won a bet that he could smoke a cigarette in the lion's cage without being mauled.

Descended from bull-baiting dogs, the Staffordshire Bull Terrier became a recognised breed by the Kennel Club in May 1935, the same year as which this blood sport was outlawed. The breed standard was decided by a group of enthusiasts at the Old Cross Guns in Cradley Heath, which originally formed part of Staffordshire until the 1974 boundary changes.

When 'Lord' George Sanger's famous circus visited Lichfield, it brought with it a menagerie of camels, zebras and other wild animals. In an interview with the *Lichfield Mercury* in April 1912, Sanger said:

Few people who visit the circus realise the amount of money that is spent upon an elephant's wardrobe. In the course of a year we spend something like £500 to provide just plain costumes for our performing animals, to say nothing about the more elaborate affairs for best wear.

One of its stars, an elephant, packed her trunk for the last time and is buried at Levetts Field.

Cannock Chase was grazed by Cannock Greyface sheep until 1904.

In 2002, four woolly rhinos were discovered in a quarry near Alrewas. One even had the remains of its last meal in its teeth. Remains of other creatures discovered at the same site included reindeer, a wolf and a horse but it was the insects that allowed the scientists studying them to calculate that when these animals lived 42,000 years ago summer temperatures in Britain would have averaged just 10°C, dropping to -22°C in winter. Professor Danielle Schreve from Royal Holloway, University of London, described the discovery as, 'the most significant fossil find of a large mammal in Britain for over 100 years', and Andy Currant, a palaeontologist from the Natural History Museum, described one of the skeletons as, 'The best example of a woolly rhino I have ever seen'.

A black calf being born amongst the white cattle at Chartley Park was a portent of a death in the Ferrers family. When the Chartley estate was sold, a bull's head was given to Stowe Village Hall where it remains on the wall.

A memorial for Burke the dog, found at Hanging Rock in the Peak District, reads: 'Beneath this Rock August 1st 1874 was buried BURKE / a noble mastiff, black and tan / faithful as woman, braver than man / A gun and a ramble his heart's desire/ with the friend of his life / the Swythamley squire'.

When wartime regulations meant that Henry Brocklehurst had to close his private zoo, he released his five Bennett's wallabies into the wilds of the Peak District. Eventually, numbers grew to around fifty, although a harsh winter in 1963 killed around half with their number reducing over the next three decades. The last photographic evidence of the wallabies was in 2009 and they are now presumed extinct, although sightings have been reported as recently as April 2015. A yak and a Nilgai antelope were also released at the same time.

Operation Rawhide was the name given to a joint attempt by the police and the army to try and round up nine Limousin cattle that escaped from a farm and disappeared into Hopwas Woods near Tamworth. Despite use of helicopters and thermal imaging equipment, the cows remained on the run for over three months.

RIVERS

The River Trent is the third longest river in the United Kingdom and takes its name from the Celtic word for trespasser, which suggests a river liable to flooding. The Romans called it Trisantona and there are claims that it dried up in the years 1101 and 1581. It appears in the name of several towns in Staffordshire locations including Burton upon Trent and Stoke-on-Trent. It rises at Biddulph in north Staffordshire and joins the Humber Estuary south of Hull, and is one of only two tidal bore rivers in England. The bore, known as the Trent Aegir, occurs when a high spring tide meets the downstream flow of the river.

The River Tame is the largest tributary of the Trent and measures 95km from its source in Oldbury to its confluence with the Trent at Alrewas in Staffordshire. The name's origins are unclear but it may mean slow moving or dark. An Anglian tribe living in its valley were known as the Tomsaete or Tame Dwellers. Although the Tame is a bigger river than the Trent, the latter is longer and is therefore considered the more senior watercourse of the two.

In the building of the Ankerside Shopping Centre in 1975 the River Anker was diverted, leading to one of the biggest ever changes in the geography of Tamworth.

In May 1908, several rivers in the county burst their banks, including the Penk, the Sow, the Trent, the Dove and the Tame, after a heavy thunderstorm added more water to watercourses already swollen by thawing stone and heavy rainfall.

The village of Elford is said to derive its name from the great number of eels that could be found in the River Tame in ancient times.

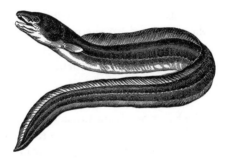

The River Manifold runs underground for part of its course, re-emerging from the Boil Holes in Ilam Park.

The River Dove takes its name from a Celtic word meaning 'dark' and for much of its 45 miles it forms a boundary between Staffordshire and Derbyshire.

In June 1831, thousands of silver coins were found on the bed of the River Dove at Tutbury by workmen improving the water supply to a nearby mill. It is thought to be the largest ever coin hoard to be found in Britain, with an estimated 360,000 coins being recovered in total. Of these, only around 1,500 are in public collections. The rest were pillaged before the authorities moved in and declared the hoard to be the property of the Crown. Further digging in the area was banned and this order still remains in force today. The hoard is believed to have belonged to Thomas of Lancaster and to have been hidden in the banks of the river shortly after his defeat at the Battle of Burton Bridge in 1322.

The River Dane was originally called the Daven, from the old Welsh meaning a 'drop' or 'trickle', implying a slow moving river. It rises around 2 miles above Three Shires Head at the point on Axe Edge Moor where Cheshire, Derbyshire and Staffordshire meet at a well-known wild swimming spot.

Rising in The Roaches, the River Churnet was used to manufacture the dyes used for the textile and silk industry in Leek. At Oakamoor, the Thomas Bolton Copper Works harnessed its power to make the world's first transatlantic telegraph cables.

The source of the River Sow is at Loggerheads, and between 1816 and 1920 the section from Stafford town centre to the Staffordshire and Worcestershire Canal at Baswich was known as the River Sow Navigation, which the Stafford Riverway Link CIC are currently working to restore. The River Sow rose to its highest level ever recorded in February 1946, causing Stafford train station to flood, with 2ft of water at the junction of Newport Road and Bridge Street and one house being washed away.

NATURE RESERVES

Allimore Green Common, a small wet grassland near Haughton in the borough of Stafford

Bateswood, a grassland reserve with a network of pools near Newcastle-under-Lyme

Black Firs and Cranberry Bog, a peatland reserve near Madeley in Newcastle-under-Lyme

Brown End Quarry, a former limestone quarry managed as a geological nature reserve near Waterhouses

Burnt Wood, an ancient oak woodland at Loggerheads

Castern Wood, a limestone grassland and ancient woodland in the Manifold Valley

Cotton Dell, an ancient woodland with a stream near Cheade

Croxall Lakes, comprising two lakes and grassland in Alrewas

Doxey Marshes, a 300-acre wetland on the edge of Stafford

Georges Hayes, ancient woodland on the edge of Cannock Chase

Harston Wood, ancient woodland in the Churnet Valley

Hem Heath Woods, woodland at Trentham

Highgate Common, ancient lowland heath near Wombourne

Ipstones Edge, a mixed site comprising of heathland, moorland and woodland

Jackson's Coppice and Marsh, semi-natural woodland near Eccleshall

Loynton Moss, a wetland landscape near Woodseaves, formed by retreating sheets of ice at the end of the last ice age

Parrot's Drumble, an ancient bluebell wood at Talke Pits, near Newcastle-under-Lyme

Pasturefields Saltmarsh, one of the last remaining inland saltmarshes in Britain, near to Hixon

Radford Meadows, river washland in Stafford

Rod Wood, wildflower meadows near Cheddleton

Side Farm Meadows, meadowland and a waterfall near Oakamoor

The Roaches, an outcrop of gritstone rocks in the Peak District

Thorswood, pastureland in the Weaver Hills

Weag's Barn, meadows and woodland near Waterhouses

9

ROYALTY AND POLITICS

ROYAL VISITS

There is a legend that Penkridge, a town south of Stafford, was once the capital of England for anywhere between two days and three years. In 958, King Edgar issued a Royal Charter describing it as a famous place and he is said to have stayed here whilst fighting for control of the Danelaw. However, its claim to being a former capital is as yet unproven.

The Mercian kings had a royal palace at Tamworth, declared to be 'the wonder of the age', although its exact location has yet to be identified. In the late eighth century, King Offa of Mercia created a defensive ditch around the town, known as Offa's Dyke, the line of which still survives in part of the town and charters show he spent Christmas AD 781 in Tamworth.

Richard II spent Christmas 1397 in Lichfield Castle, consuming 200 tuns of wine and 2,000 oxen. Two years later, the king's fortunes had changed and he was imprisoned in Lichfield on route from Chester to London. Some accounts say he was incarcerated in Lichfield Castle, others specify a tower in the fortified Cathedral Close, likely to have been the north-east tower. In some accounts of the story it is reported that Richard made an unsuccessful attempt to escape through a window.

In 1402, Henry IV ordered 'knights, squires, and yeomen from various parts of the country to meet him at Lichfield for his campaign against Owain Glyn Dŵr.

Queen Margaret of Anjou is said to have watched the Battle of Blore Heath from the tower of St Mary's Church at Mucklestone with her son Prince Henry. After seeing her troops defeated she ordered William Skelhorn the blacksmith to reverse her horses shoes to disguise her escape. Some accounts say that Skelhorn was then executed on his own anvil in a bid to preserve his silence. The anvil can still be seen in the churchyard with the inscription, 'This anvil came from the smithy when it was demolished and is believed to have been used by William Skelhorn in 1459'. Her footprints may not remain imprinted on the stone floor, as legend would have it, but there is stained glass here recalling the event.

Mary, Queen of Scots was held captive at several sites in Staffordshire. In January 1569, she was taken to Tutbury Castle and at Christmas 1585 she was moved to the manor house at Chartley. Whilst out riding, she was arrested and kept at Tixall Hall for around two weeks, whilst her rooms at Chartley were searched for evidence of the conspiracy that would later become known as the 'Babington Plot'. On being taken from Tixall back to Chartley, she met some poor people at the gate and wept as she told them, 'I have nothing for you. I am a beggar as well as you, all is taken from me'. Based on the evidence discovered in the queen's room at Chartley, it was decided that she should stand trial, and on 21 September 1586 she began her final journey to Fotheringhay Castle in Northamptonshire, with stops at Abbots Bromley and Burton upon Trent en route.

Elizabeth I visited Stafford in 1575 and addressed concerns regarding the town's troubled capping industry and the absence of the assizes, factors which she was told were contributing to the economic decay of the town. This was the furthest north the queen travelled in her reign of 44 years and 127 days. During her time in Staffordshire, the queen was entertained at Chartley Hall, the home of Robert Devereux, 2nd Earl of Essex and also visited Lichfield on 27 July, and there are records of the 'Charges when the Queene's Matie was at the Cyttye of Lich', which include payments for trumpeters, horses and paving, mending the market cross and guildhall, and a sum was paid to 'Wm Hollcroft, for kepynge Madde Richard when her Matie was here'.

Charles I stayed at the Ancient High House in Stafford on 17 and 18 September 1643 with his nephew Prince Rupert of the Rhine, attending the nearby St Mary's Church, when flowers were strewn along his route. When the king and his nephew were walking in the garden of the house, Price Rupert put two shots through the tail of the weathercock of the same church in order to demonstrate to the king the accuracy of a new continental horse pistol. Since 1986, the house has been a museum with each room decorated to represent historical eras and the Staffordshire Yeomanry Museum, founded in 1794, is based in the attics.

King James visited Tamworth Castle with Prince Charles in 1619 and marks on stonework and doors are believed to be 'witch marks', designed to protect the building and its inhabitants from evil and supposedly added to the castle at the king's request. On later tours of Staffordshire, James stayed at Wychnor Hall in August 1621, returning again in August 1624.

Grand Duke Michael Mikhailovich had been exiled from Russia by his cousin, Tsar Alexander III, and in 1900 he rented Keele Hall. When visiting Mikhailovich, King Edward VII became the first ruling monarch to stay at Keele. The town council of

Newcastle under Lyme awarded Mikhailovich the honour of Lord High Steward of the Borough.

In the early hours of 8 September 1651, Charles II arrived at Moseley Old Hall in Staffordshire, looking for a place to hide and a new escape route. He was met at the back door by owner Thomas Whitgreave and the family priest John Huddleston, who gave up his four-poster bed and shared his hiding place with the future king when Cromwell's soldiers came seeking him. By the mid twentieth century, Moseley Old Hall was suffering from neglect and subsidence. This 'atmospheric Elizabethan farmhouse that saved a King' was itself saved by the National Trust, when they took over in 1962.

One prized relic from the time of Charles II's great escape was a rag he had used to mop up a nosebleed. Father Huddleston passed this 'bloody clout' to a Mrs Braithwaite who kept it as a remedy for the king's evil, another name given to the disease known as scrofula. The tradition of 'touching for the king's evil', was continued by King James II who carried out a 'touching' ceremony at Lichfield Cathedral in 1687. The last English monarch to partake in the ritual was Queen Anne, who 'touched' 2-year-old Samuel Johnson at one of the ceremonies in 1712. The touch piece or coin, which the queen presented young Samuel with, which he is said to have worn throughout his life, is now in the British Museum.

When the Prince of Wales, later Kind Edward VIII, visited the Branston Artificial Silk Company in Branston, he was presented with an artificial silk scarf embroidered with his initials and white ostrich feathers.

In 1834, Queen Victoria and Prince Albert visited Drayton Manor, the home of Robert Peel. Two roads leading from the railway station in Tamworth, where they arrived for their visit, are named after them.

In 1931, Captain Fielden flew the Price of Wales, later Edward VIII, from Windsor to Meir, to open the outpatients department at Rosemary Ednam Memorial Hospital at Hartshill. On his return journey, Fielden was forced to make an emergency landing at Fulford, near Blythe Bridge. The hospital was named after Lady Rosemary Ednam, daughter of the Duke of Sutherland, who had been fundraising to build an extension at the hospital when she was killed in a plane crash the previous year. The prince had proposed to Rosemary in 1918 but his father opposed the marriage.

George Fox, who bought Elmhurst Hall in 1875, died in London from a chill in 1894 after moving from Elmhurst to enable the Duke of Sutherland to use the house to host the Prince of Wales on his visit to Lichfield for the centenary of the Staffordshire Yeomanry.

ROYAL CONNECTIONS

Leofric, Earl of Mercia most famous for being the husband of Lady Godiva, died in 1057 at his estate in King's Bromley and was buried at Coventry.

Reginald Pole, son of Margaret, 8th Countess of Salisbury and Sir Richard Pole, was born at Stourton Castle on 12 March 1500. He was offered the Archbishopric of York by Henry VIII, provided he would support the king's divorce from Catherine of Aragon. Unable to do so, Pole travelled to Padua from where he sent Henry a document denouncing his claim for supremacy over the English Church and defending the authority of the Pope. In December 1536, Pole was made a cardinal and was enlisted by the Pope to persuade the Catholic monarchs of Europe to rally against the king. By way of revenge for an act he considered treason, Henry executed Pole's brother and mother. When Mary I ascended the throne, Pole returned to England and in March 1556, he was appointed Archbishop of Canterbury. He died on 17 November 1558, around twelve hours after the death of the queen.

As the judge who presided over the court at the trial of Charles I, John Bradshaw, steward of Newcastle-under-Lyme, was the first man to sign the king's death warrant. He was later appointed president of the Council of State and elected MP for Stafford in 1654 (although he declined to take up the seat, refusing to recognise the new government). On his deathbed he said that if asked to try the king again, he would be the first man to do it. Following the Restoration, his body was exhumed from Westminster Abbey, hanged at Tyburn, and his head displayed on a spike at Westminster.

Another Staffordshire signatory was Thomas Harrison, son of the Mayor of Newcastle-under-Lyme and the seventeenth man to add his name to the warrant. When he was hung, drawn and quartered for treason in October 1660, Samuel Pepys recorded the execution in his diary:

> I went out to Charing Cross, to see Major-general Harrison hanged, drawn, and quartered; which was done there, he looking as cheerful as any man could do in that condition. He

was presently cut down, and his head and heart shown to the people, at which there was great shouts of joy ...

Thomas Parker was born in Leek in July 1666. When Queen Anne died in August 1714, her successor the elector of Hanover was in Germany and so Parker was acting regent of Great Britain, Ireland and the realms beyond the seas until the new king could take the crown. In 1718, Parker delivered the king's speech in the House of Lords, as the monarch did not speak English. He was appointed Lord Chancellor in the same year. Three years later, Parker was given the title Earl of Macclesfield. He financed the building of Leek Grammar School in 1723 shortly before being impeached for fraud – convicted of taking more than £100,000 in bribes. The scandal forced his resignation as Lord Chancellor, and Parker spent six weeks in the Tower of London until he could raise sufficient funds to pay the £30,000 he had been fined for his financial misconduct. Following his disgrace, Parker's appearances in public were rare, one notable exception being to act as one of the pallbearers at the funeral of Sir Isaac Newton in 1727.

Athelstan established a total of nineteen royal mints including ones at Stafford and Tamworth. A collection of coins struck at the latter are on display in the castle museum.

Elias Ashmole, founder of the Oxford Museum, was born in Breadmarket Street, Lichfield, in 1617. Ashmole attended the city's grammar school and was also a chorister at the cathedral. After the Restoration, Ashmole was appointed Windsor Herald by Charles II, and was also a founder member of the Royal Society.

A fictitious plot fabricated by Titus Oates, alleging there was a Catholic conspiracy to assassinate Charles II, led to the executions of a number of innocent men before the deception became apparent. Stephen Dugdale, a steward to Walter Aston of Tixall Hall, gave 'evidence' at the trial of Lord Stafford – stating that he had heard talk of slaying the king at Tixall and that Lord Stafford had not only been present but had also offered him £500 to carry out the crime. Stafford was beheaded on 29 December 1680. Walter Aston, who had been imprisoned in the Tower of London, was never brought to trial and Oates' web of lies eventually unravelled. When James II ascended the throne, Oates was tried and found guilty of perjury. He was sentenced to life imprisonment and to be 'whipped through the streets of London five days a year for the remainder of his life', although he was later pardoned by William and Mary.

POLITICAL PROTESTS

The North Staffs Miners' Wives action group was formed in 1985 in the wake of the Miners' Strike to give support to sacked miners and their families. A camp was set up outside Trentham, Colliery, the last local deep pit in north Staffordshire, as part of a campaign to save it from closure. The No. 2 pit shaft was occupied for three days by three of the women, Brenda Proctor, Bridget Bell and Gina Earl. Outside the pit, a fourth woman, Rose Hunter, maintained communications between the women and the outside world. Eventually, the women agreed to leave to be met, as they exited, by Arthur Scargill. The last symbol of coalmining in Stoke-on-Trent was the pithead winding gear 'A' frame, which gave the mine its local name of 'The Big A'; it was demolished on 19 August 1997.

The 1842 Pottery Riots, which largely took place in Hanley and Burslem, were prompted by the decision of a Longton mine owner to reduce the pay of his workers by almost a shilling a day without the statutory fortnight's notice. The men went on strike and were supported by other miners in the area. By the end of July strikes were taking place across the region and Thomas Powys, a magistrate from Burslem and deputy lord lieutenant of

Staffordshire, ordered troops to fire on a procession of strikers in Burslem Square, killing one man and injuring many more. In retaliation, the crowd burned down Powys' house and carried out other acts of vandalism and revenge. Over the course of the day, arrests were made, with 274 people eventually being brought to trial. The man killed in Burslem Square is supposedly buried in St John's graveyard in the town. However, despite the following epitaph, which seems to allude to the events, 'I went up town a sight to see/Met with a shot that killed me/ No mourn for me I beg you make/But love my sister for my sake', Nathaniel Johnson who is buried here died in 1837 and cannot therefore have been the man shot that day.

In 1783, a canal boat carrying supplies of flour and cheese for the people of the Potteries arrived at the wharf near the Josiah Wedgewood pottery. The owners, realising they could demand a higher price in a big city, decided to continue to Manchester. However, news had started to spread and a large crowd followed the boat to Longport, eventually taking control of the vessel and bringing it back to Etruria where Stephen Barlow and Joseph Boulton sold the provisions to the assembled crowd at a reduced price. A second boat arrived and its cargo was also distributed in the same way. As more people arrived, troops were sent to dispatch the mob, which eventually dispersed. Singled out as leaders, Barlow and Boulton were arrested and charged with inciting a riot, damaging property and theft. Barlow was found guilty and hanged whereas Boulton 'escaped' with a public flogging.

NOTABLE STAFFORDSHIRE MPS

Jack Ashley was MP for Stoke-on-Trent South for twenty-six years, from 1966 to 1992. In December 1967, Ashley lost his hearing as a result of complications from a routine operation to correct a perforated eardrum. He was persuaded to retain his seat in the House of Commons, electing instead to take a crash course in lip reading. He thus became the first totally deaf MP.

Ashley was a lifelong campaigner for the disabled, especially the deaf and blind. He led high-profile campaigns, including the campaign for improved compensation for victims of thalidomide, vaccine damage and damage done by the arthritis drug Opren. In 1986, he and his wife founded the charity Defeating Deafness. Following his retirement from Parliament in 1992, Ashley was made Baron Ashley of Stoke.

Robert Peel was the son of a textile entrepreneur who followed in his father's footsteps to become the MP for Tamworth. His initial contribution to debate in the House of Commons was described by the speaker as 'the best first speech since that of William Pitt'. Whilst on holiday in Rome in November 1834, Peel was asked by William IV to be prime minster, following the dismissal of the Whig government by the king. Peel called a general election and, at the family home of Drayton Manor, penned the Tamworth Manifesto, the first ever party political election manifesto, setting out, 'A declaration of the general principles and views of the Government which I have been asked to form'. Despite Tories being outnumbered by Whigs, Peel was asked by the king to form an administration, but after being outvoted in the House of Commons on several occasions, he resigned on 8 April 1835. Peel was again asked to form a Conservative Administration in August 1841, but the repeal of the Corn Laws in 1846 split the party and Peel resigned once more. On 29 June 1850, Peel was thrown from his horse on Constitution Hill in London and died three days later from his injuries. Although Peel was offered a state burial in Westminster Abbey, he had requested to be buried in the village of Drayton.

Jennie Lee was elected MP for Cannock in 1945, and held the seat until defeat in the 1970 election. On 5 November 1970, she was made Baroness Asheridge. Lee was the daughter of a coal miner and was first elected to the House of Commons in 1929 when she won the seat for the MP for North Lanarkshire. In 1964, Lee was appointed the first Minister for Arts in Harold

Wilson's government and during this time government funding for the arts doubled and the Open University was founded. Lee was married to fellow MP and Labour Party leader Aneurin 'Nye' Bevan.

Historian and broadcaster Tristram Hunt was elected as the MP for Stoke-on-Trent Central in the 2010 general election. Hunt served as Shadow Secretary of State for Education until September 2015 when Jeremy Corbyn was elected as Labour leader.

10

FOLKLORE AND TRADITIONS

CUSTOMS AND TRADITIONS

Robin Hood is most often associated with Nottinghamshire but there are those who believe he was a Staffordshire man. A ballad called 'The Birth of Robin Hood' is set at Tutbury Castle, and there are also claims that he was born at Loxley near Uttoxeter. A horn kept at Loxley Hall with the initials R.H. and known as Robin Hood's horn has also helped to perpetuate the myth. Elford Lowe, near the village of the same name, and another Lowe around a mile away, are known as Robin Hood's Shooting Butts, with local folklore suggesting he sometimes practised here and was able to fire an arrow from one to the other.

Every New Year's Day, the Lord of Essington would bring a goose to Hilton Hall, drive it three times around the fire, carry it into the kitchen and deliver it to the cook. Essington would then present the dressed bird to the Lord of Hilton and receive a dish of meat in return. The fire was blown using 'Jack of Hilton', a small and hollow brass man, kneeling down with his right hand above his head and his left hand holding his penis. Water was poured through the hole in Jack's back and, once heated over the fire, the water would evaporates from a hole in Jack's mouth in a blast of steam. Although the custom at Hilton is believed to be unique, a similar figure to Jack was once owned by Mr à Court Repington of Amington Hall in Tamworth.

The tradition of beating the bounds was observed by Lichfield Cathedral choristers each Ascension Day. Accompanied by members of the clergy, the boys would begin opposite St Mary's Vicarage and stop off at several places: 'midway between the pool and Gaia Lane', 'the Bishop's kitchen garden', 'the Dean's kitchen garden', 'Milley's Hospital', 'the boundary stone on the Minster Pool Bridge' and 'the Verger's house in the corner of the Close'. Finally the procession would halt at the old pump to the north-west of the cathedral, to which water from the Conduit Head up at Maple Hayes once flowed along a lead pipe. The boys would carry elm boughs, and at each of the stop-off points there was a reading from the scriptures and a verse of a hymn was sung. In 1936, the elm boughs were brought inside the cathedral and laid on the font. An account from 1910 describes how choristers would collect boughs from the Dimbles area of the city before returning to the close and decorating the houses. In recent years, the tradition has been replaced by choristers singing from the roof of the cathedral.

Two maidens' garlands, made of faded paper flowers and gloves, which were once white, hang at the church of the Holy Cross in Ilam. They would originally have been made to be placed upon the coffin of a young woman from the parish who had met with a tragic end, and afterwards hung on display in the church.

Wychnor Hall was home to an unusual marital custom that began in the reign of Edward III. If a couple were still happily married after a year and a day, they could go to the hall, accompanied by neighbours who were prepared to testify to their marital bliss. After the husband had sworn under oath that he 'would not have changed for none other, farer ne fowler, richer ne powrer, ne for none other descended of gretter lynage, slepyng ne waking, at noo tyme; and if the seid X were sole, and I sole, I wolde take her to be my wife before all the wymen of the worlde, of what condytions soevere they be, good or evyle, as helpe me God, and his seyntys, and this flesh, and all fleshes', the couple were presented with a flitch of bacon.

The records show that only three couples were ever awarded the bacon. The first couple argued so much over it on the way out, they had to give it straight back. The second couple hadn't seen each other since their wedding day, as the husband was a seaman, and the third couple were described as 'a good-natured man and his dumb wife'. According to *The Spectator* in 1714, one couple applied soon after their honeymoon but it was deemed that insufficient time since their marriage had elapsed and they were sent away with just one rasher of bacon. By the second half of the eighteenth century, the custom had demised and the flitch was replaced by a picture carved into the wood above the fireplace in the main hall.

In 1846, the village of Flash, the highest village in England, established the Flash Loyal Union Friendly Society nicknamed The Teapot Club. Although the tradition of villagers collecting spare coins in their teapots for distribution to other locals who fell on hard times ended in 1995 due to the introduction of new laws on savings organisations, the annual Teapot Parade, where a large model teapot is carried through the village, continues. A well-dressing ceremony has also been added to the festivities in recent years.

Each year, on the first Monday following the first Sunday after 4 September, the Abbots Bromley Horn Dancers – made up of six deer men, a fool, a hobby horse, a bowman and a Maid Marian – collect the set of ancient horns from the church of St Nicholas at 8 a.m. They perform their dance at locations in and around the village of Abbots Bromley, including the lawn in front of Blithfield Hall, before returning the horns to the church twelve hours later. Whether the dance began as a pagan fertility ritual or is to do with hunting rights no one really knows, but the mystery surrounding its origins is part of the tradition's appeal. Although the dance is performed at various locations outside Abbots Bromley throughout the year, a second set of horns are kept for this purpose. The original horns never leave the village and are kept at the church for 364 days a year. One story told by Jack Brown of the English Folk Dance and Song Society is that in the nineteenth century, the dancers took a set of elk horns dancing in Burton and, having consumed quite a lot of rum, managed to lose them. According to some, the horns were stolen, whilst others say the dancers decided they were too heavy and deposited them into the River Trent so they didn't have to carry them all the way back to Abbots Bromley!

Before it was banned by the Duke of Devonshire in the eighteenth century, bull running took place in Tutbury each year. A bull with its ears and tail cropped, horns cut off, smeared with soap and with pepper blown up its nose was chased through the streets of Tutbury. If the bull escaped over the bridge into Derbyshire, he remained the property of the prior. If caught, he became the property of the minstrels.

The Lichfield Bower is held every year on the spring bank holiday in May and dates back to 1145 when Henry II issued a statute ordering all towns and cities to hold a Court of Array where all the men capable of bearing arms should muster once a year. A bower house was erected at Greenhill and decorated with greenery and the city's men-at-arms paraded through the streets before being fed and watered. They were joined in the procession by Morris dancers and people carrying figures of saints draped in garlands known as posies. Although the need to hold a Court of Array ceased in 1690, the citizens of Lichfield kept up the tradition adapting and adding to it over the centuries. At dawn on Bower Day in 1952, some of the male residents of Lower Sandford Street were gathering elm branches near to Beacon Farm, on the edge of what is now Beacon Park. Apparently every year, for as long as anyone could remember, the boughs had been cut from the trees and used to decorate the houses in 'Old San' as the street was known. However, as the men gathered the boughs, a police officer arrived and instructed them to stop on the orders of the town clerk and the Estates Committee of the City Council, as it had been reported that in previous years the trees had been damaged. The residents of 'Old San' were angry that their ancient privilege was being threatened and sent a message back to the town clerk and mayor, Cllr C. Bridgeman, that if no further boughs were allowed to be cut then those that had already been collected would be used to barricade Sandford Street and prevent the Bower Procession from entering. As tensions rose, the town clerk and the mayor arrived at the scene and gave their permission for residents to continue collecting boughs, providing that no trees were damaged in the process. The boughs were then used to decorate the houses of old Sandford Street along with bunting, balloons and slogans, with prizes awarded for the best decorated properties.

The Sheriff's Ride is an annual perambulation of the boundary of the city (and between 1553 and 1888 the county) of Lichfield on the Saturday nearest to the feast of the Nativity of the Blessed Virgin Mary, aka 8 September. The ride of around 16 miles traditionally began (and ended) at Cross in Hand Lane, where a long-since vanished cross indicated the city limits but now it starts at the guildhall. The purpose of the ride was for the sheriff to inspect the boundaries of the city and, at one time, a member of each household was required to participate, with senior citizens passing on their knowledge of the boundaries, which could be called upon in times of dispute. In 1656, there was a disagreement over where Lichfield ended and Lord Paget's land began (and vice versa) and evidence was given by four city elders regarding the line of the boundary they had followed each year since they were boys.

THINGS THAT GO BUMP
IN STAFFORDSHIRE

Paranormal activity has been reported at both the former RAF Lichfield site, where a headless airman who died after walking into the propeller of his plane has been sighted in one of the former hangars, and at RAF Tatenhill where the sounds of young men are heard in disused buildings and old-fashioned aftershave can be smelled in the corner of one particular warehouse at 8.30 every evening.

At midnight, the Blake Mere mermaid rises from her pool to entice single men travelling along the road between Leek and Buxton to a watery grave. One version of the mermaid's tale is that a sailor from the nearby village of Thorncliffe fell in love with her and brought her back to landlocked Staffordshire from the sea like a goldfish won at a fair, which may explain her animosity towards single men. A more sinister explanation for her presence is that she was once a young woman who rejected the advances of a local man called Joshua Linnet. Hell hath no fury like a man scorned, and he accused her of being a witch, convincing some of the other locals to drown her in the pool. Three days later he was found dead in the water, his face clawed to pieces. There was a reported sighting of the mermaid in the mid nineteenth century when locals apparently began to drain the pool in an attempt to discover whether it truly was bottomless. Their antics supposedly incurred the wrath of the watery wraith, causing her to get up from her lakebed before midnight to warn them that she'd flood nearby Leek and Leekfrith if they didn't stop immediately.

A phantom black dog is seen on the lane at the Hermitage on the way to Ipstones.

Broughton Hall near Eccleshall has a ghost known as Red Socks. A woman scrubbing the Long Gallery stairs one day looked up from her cleaning and saw a young man in red stockings. She moved her bucket out of the way so he could pass but he walked right through her. The ghost is said to have been a young boy who lived at the hall who was shot by passing parliamentarians when he leaned from the window shouting, 'I am for the King!' The hall is also said to carry a curse that no elder son will inherit the property.

A headless horseman is said to haunt the village of Onecote. In 1900, a farmer returning from Leek reported that he had been pulled onto the back of a phantom horse by a headless rider and taken on a terrifying journey across fields and hedgerows. Close to home, the farmer was flung to the ground and died of his injuries a few days after. Some believe it is the ghost of a murdered pedlar, others suggest it is the ghost of a knight killed in battle against the Scots, but perhaps the most sinister explanation of all is that it is one of four spirits cast out of heaven and forced to roam the Earth until the Day of Judgement. Whatever the explanation, attempts to exorcise the ghost have failed and so the headless horseman of Onecote rides on.

A churchwarden from Leek used soil from the churchyard to grow vegetables and as a result one of the radishes they grew was possessed with the soul of the deceased from whose grave the earth had been taken. As the churchwarden's wife pulled the radish from the soil it screamed and begged to be returned to the graveyard. The soil was returned and from then on the churchwarden sourced his compost eslewhere.

Ye Olde Windmill at Gentleshaw is haunted by two young children, killed after falling through a trapdoor inside the mill, which now stands derelict in the beer garden. The long-vanished trapdoor is sometimes heard to slam shut. Two flour-covered children have been seen playing in the area and sometimes on a snowy day two sets of little footprints can be seen circling the base of the mill.

Bessy Banks Grave was an area of Lichfield where, according to local legend, a young woman had taken her own life. Anna Seward penned a poem about the tragedy from what she described as 'the grave of a suicide' and David Garrick also described the places as supposedly haunted. The story is also the subject of a poem by Frederick Price, although in his version Bessy is drowned. The name survived until at least the early twentieth century but the name and the story are now all but lost.

Stafford Castle was once reported to be haunted by a headless horseman, something that had apparently been witnessed by the resident caretakers at the site. However, on investigating, it was discovered that the supposed paranormal activity was in fact a group of escaped cows!

Weston Hall near Stafford was used by the army during the Second World War, but the Auxiliary Territorial Service (ATS) girls stationed there found it so unnerving that they preferred to sleep outside in tents rather than inside the house itself. Whilst carrying out restoration work in the 1990s, workmen refused to go to the hall alone. The hall is said to be haunted by a Green Lady, a White Lady and a Grey Lady.

WITCHES AND WIZARDRY

A cave beneath a house at Seisdon, known as Tinker's Castle, was once occupied by a hermit who supplied local girls with love potions.

In 2009, archaeologists excavating the Tipping Street car park in Stafford discovered a seventeenth-century Bellarmine jar on the site of the former Turk's Head pub. The vessel is believed to have been used as a witch bottle, to deter evil spirits.

Factory women from the Potteries would often touch iron for luck if they met a clergyman on their way to work.

A piece of hawthorn picked by someone else and brought to you could be hung in the rafters of the house to protect against fire.

When the church at Hulton Abbey was demolished, the tombs of James de Audley and his wife were discovered in front of the high altar. On opening the tombs, it was found that the lady's hair had continued to grow after death.

A drowning pool for women charged with witchcraft is said to have existed on the site now occupied by the Swan Hotel in Stafford.

In the towns and villages around Needwood, burning elder wood was believed to summon the Devil, hence the local saying, 'If you do, you will bring the Old Lad on top of the chimney'. It was reported that on one occasion at Newborough a young boy present cried out with fright when he saw people throwing elder onto a fire as he believed that the devil would be down the chimney in a minute.

The people of Staffordshire believed that burning fern brought rain, and so Charles I asked his chamberlain to write to the sheriff to forbid its burning whilst he was passing through the county.

At Eccleshall, a piece of Hawthorn gathered on Ascension Day and hung in the rafters of a house would protect the property from being struck by lightning.

When an oak tree at an old deer park in Hanbury was struck by lightning, people came from miles around to take pieces of the wood to use as charms to protect their houses from a similar misfortune.

Three knocks are always heard at Comberford Hall before the death of a family member.

The Staffordshire witch brooch was heart shaped with unequal sides made of silver and set with eighteen crystals. Witch brooches were believed to protect against all forms of evil and these pieces of jewellery were often bought at the same time as a wedding ring.

A pair of mole's feet carried in the pocket of an old man from Wheaton Aston as a cure against toothache are on display in the Pitt Rivers Museum in Oxford.

A well at Brown Edge was sunk at a site discovered by divining for water.

When an old woman was found drowned in her well at Eccleshall in 1876, the body was laid out on the ground. The grass where the corpse had rested turned a peculiar green and her neighbours believed this proved that she had died by foul means.

Staffordshire's most famous alleged witch is Molly Leigh, a woman from Burslem, ostracised from society and often blamed when anything went wrong. Molly made an enemy of Parson

Spencer of St John's in Burslem for refusing to attend church, and the animosity escalated when the local vicar accused her of sending her pet blackbird to sit on the sign of his favourite pub and turning the beer sour. When Molly died in 1748, Spencer buried her in the churchyard, but when there were reports of her pet blackbird making a nuisance of itself in the town the parson assembled a group of men to visit Molly's cottage. Through the window they convinced themselves they'd spotted her sitting in her rocking chair knitting. Deciding that her spirit must be properly laid to rest, they returned to the churchyard at night, opened up her grave into which they placed her pet bird and realigned the grave from the usual east-west alignment, to a north-south one. However, it is said that despite Parson Spencer's best efforts, the ghost of Molly Leigh can be summoned once again by circling her grave three times and chanting 'Molly Leigh, Molly Leigh, chase me round the apple tree'.

11

WAR IN STAFFORDSHIRE

HISTORIC BATTLES

On 13 November 1002, Aethelred the Unready ordered the killing of all Danes in the kingdom. The extent to which the king's instructions were carried out is not known, but there is a story that a massacre of Danes did take place at Hound Hill in Marchington.

A place near Checkley is known as Naked Field, after the unclothed and unburied bodies from a battle that supposedly took place there.

At the Battle of Stafford in 1069 the Mercians, supported by Welsh soldiers, rebelled against the invading Normans. It took the arrival of William the Conqueror himself to suppress the uprising and defeat the rebels. William returned the following year and to make sure it didn't happen again the town was decimated. Robert, the son of William's standard bearer, Roger de Toeni, built Stafford Castle and took the town's name as his own to demonstrate to the locals exactly who was in charge.

Legend has it that in 1403, two feuding neighbours from opposite sides of the River Trent set out to fight on opposite sides at the Battle of Shrewsbury. Sir William Handsacre was for the rebel Sir Henry 'Hotspur' Percy and loyal to King Henry IV was Sir Robert Mavesyn, whose name was said to derive from the French *malvoisin*, meaning 'dangerous neighbour'. At

Bridge Meadow, near to the site of High Bridge, it's believed that the paths of the two enemies crossed, as did their swords. Living up to his name, Mavesyn killed Handsacre but his victory was short-lived and he met his end at the Battle of Shrewsbury, 'standing with the King and fighting by his side even unto death', if the epitaph on his tombstone in the church of St Nicholas at Mavesyn Ridware is to be believed. When the church of St John the Baptist in Armitage was rebuilt in the mid nineteenth century, a stone coffin was discovered in the north wall. Inside was a skeleton with a full set of teeth and a sword. Local tradition had it that these were the mortal remains of Sir William Handsacre.

Walter Devereux, Lord Ferrers of Chartley was killed at the Battle of Bosworth fighting for Richard III.

Ten knights killed at the Battle of Blore Heath on 23 September 1459 are said to be buried in a mound in the Langot Valley, with their faces looking towards the river.

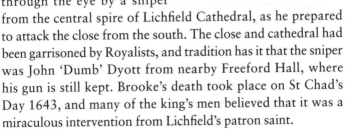

Brooke House on Dam Street in Lichfield is named after Lord Brooke, a general of the parliamentarian forces who was killed by a shot through the eye by a sniper from the central spire of Lichfield Cathedral, as he prepared to attack the close from the south. The close and cathedral had been garrisoned by Royalists, and tradition has it that the sniper was John 'Dumb' Dyott from nearby Freeford Hall, where his gun is still kept. Brooke's death took place on St Chad's Day 1643, and many of the king's men believed that it was a miraculous intervention from Lichfield's patron saint.

During the Civil War, Bishop of Lichfield Robert Wright was released on bail from the Tower of London, where he'd been imprisoned with eleven other bishops, to return to his palace at Eccleshall Castle. He died of a heart attack there in early 1643 but could not be buried as the castle was under siege from the parliamentarians. When Royalist soldiers arrived at Eccleshall, fresh from their victory at Hopton Heath, they attempted to bury the bishop. However, Roundheads heading from Stafford met them and a battle was fought in the High Street. Cromwell's men won, and took the castle.

In 1651, following the Battle of Worcester, the Duke of Buckingham was being pursued through the Langot Valley by Roundhead troops. He escaped by hiding in the brick oven of a cottage called Armsdale whilst the woman who lived there scattered the kitchen with flour, to give the impression she had been baking. When the soldiers came to search the house she begged them not to open the oven and spoil her batch of bread. When the troops left, the woman arranged for the duke to exchange clothes with a labourer and he was taken to a cave overlooking the valley near Blore Pipe, which is now known as Buckingham's Hole. The entrance could only be reached by a rope and the duke is said to have slipped and broken his arm. After several days in the cave, the duke continued his escape to London via Nottingham.

Henry Paget was famously hit by a cannon shot at the Battle of Waterloo and is said to have exclaimed, 'By God sir, I've lost my leg', to which the Duke of Wellington apparently replied, 'By God sir, so you have!' The shattered limb was amputated at the nearby house of Monsieur Hyacinthe Joseph-Maris Paris and the saw used in the operation is on display at the National Army Museum. Monsieur Paris asked if the amputated leg could be buried in his garden. Paget agreed and the leg was given its own headstone, which read: 'Here lies the leg of the illustrious and valiant Earl Uxbridge, Lieutenant General of his Britannic

Majesty. Commander in Chief of the English, Belgian and Dutch cavalry, wounded on the 18 June 1815 at the memorable battle of Waterloo, who, by his heroism, assisted in the triumph of the cause of mankind, gloriously decided by the resounding victory of the said day.' Back home, Paget was a hero, and was given the title Marquess of Anglesey by the Prince Regent. He died of a stroke on 29 April 1854 and was buried in a vault below Lichfield Cathedral.

During the Jacobite rebellion, as retreating soldiers walked over Lask Edge, a drummer who wandered away from his companions was shot by an English infantryman. The hill where the death took place is known as Drummer's Knob or Cob.

In the 1860s, the War Office is said to have considered moving the country's arsenal from Woolwich to Cannock Chase due to its central location and good network links, but the plan never came to fruition.

THE FIRST AND SECOND WORLD WARS

During the Second World War, a series of pillboxes were built along the Western Command Defensive Line No. 5, and a complete line survives in the section running from south to north on the west bank of the River Tame, near Hopwas, although the accompanying trenches and barbed wire defences have long since vanished. Pillbox UORN 5336 can be found on a front lawn on a housing estate near to the river and two further type-24 pillboxes can be found to the north of Hopwas Bridge. A surviving list of the pillboxes in each area describes how each of them was camouflaged, with the help of an ash heap, a woodman's cottage, a cowshed and haystacks.

During the Second World War, the Home Guard stationed as lookouts on the tower of St Lawrence in Bramshall rang the bells to signify that the Germans had invaded after mistakenly identifying some parachutists.

Sir Robert Peel, 5th Baronet of Drayton Manor, absconded from Harrow School and joined the army during the First World War, giving a false age. His son Robert, 6th baronet and the last of the Tamworth line of Peels, was one of fifteen men who died on board HMS *Tenedos* when it took a direct hit from Japanese bombers in Columbo Harbour on Easter Sunday 1942.

Three and a half miles of tunnels were excavated beneath the sandstone hills of Kinver during the Second World War, to create an underground shadow factory, where the Rover car company could manufacture aeroplane engines and components, safe from the bombs of the enemy. The site was later developed as a cold war bunker, designed to act as one of the thirteen Regional Seats of Government from where the country would operate from in the event of a nuclear attack on Britain. Since 1993, the complex has been in the hands of the Drakelow Tunnels Preservation Trust who intend to transform it into the largest cold war complex in the country and regular open days and tours are held, making it the largest underground space in the UK to be open to the general public.

In autumn 1914, construction of two military camps, Brocton and Rugeley, began on Lord Lichfield's estate on Cannock Chase. Over 100 men were employed in the project. The camps were made up of wooden huts adapted for use as barracks, mess rooms and workshops. Work on erecting the first huts began in March 1915 and the first battalions arrived soon after. The camps were initially used as transit centres for soldiers en-route to the Western Front but later became a training facility. Over 40,000 men could be accommodated at the camps and the New Zealand Rifle Brigade based their UK headquarters there. It is estimated that more than 500,000 soldiers were trained in subjects such as musketry, signalling, physical training and gas warfare at Cannock Chase during the First World War. When the war ended, the huts were sold off and used for a variety of uses in towns and villages across the area. A hut used as a parish hall and meeting house in the village of Gayton until 2006, was moved to the Friends of Cannock Chase Museum where it is now used as an interpretation and education centre for the nearby Great War Camps.

THE STAFFORDSHIRE REGIMENT'S VICTORIA CROSSES

Since its creation in 1856, the Victoria Cross, Britain's highest recognition for bravery, has been awarded to the Staffordshire Regiment thirteen times.

Drummer Thomas Flynn VC
Severely injured in the successful charge against a mutineer gun battery at Cawnpore on 28 November 1857, Flynn continued to fight hand to hand against two of the enemy.

Private Samuel Wassall VC
During the Battle of Isandhlwana on 22 January 1879, Wassall was part of a mounted infantry overwhelmed by Zulus. As Wassall rode his horse towards the Buffalo River to escape, he saw a comrade drowning and successfully rescued him under enemy fire.

Sergeant Anthony Clarke Booth VC
Booth was with a company of the 80th Regiment on the banks of the Intombi River when, on 12 March 1879, they were attacked by Zulus. Booth rallied the survivors and conducted their retreat for 3 miles.

Sergeant John Carmichael VC
During the third Battle of Ypres on 8 September 1917, Carmichael was leading a working party in a trench near Hill 60. When one of the men dislodged and activated a grenade, Carmichael shouted a warning to the others before placing his helmet over the grenade and standing on it, suffering injuries but saving the lives of his men.

Lieutenant Colonel Edward Ellers Delaval Henderson VC
Henderson led his battalion against Turkish positions at Kut Al Amara on 25 January 1917, but was wounded and forced to withdraw. On leading a second attack, he was wounded again and eventually captured the position by a bayonet charge. Before being evacuated Henderson was wounded twice more and died shortly afterwards.

Captain John Franks Vallentin VC
Whilst temporarily commanding an attack on a trench near Ypres, on 7 November 1914, Vallentin was wounded but continued and was later killed by machine-gun fire.

Lance-Corporal William Harold Coltman VC, DCM MM
During the assault on the Hindenburg Line in October 1918,

Coltman went out into the open three times during a German counter-attack to give first aid to wounded men and carry them to safety. As a result of his heroism, Coltman is the most decorated other rank in the British Army.

Private Thomas Barrett VC
In the Ypres Salient on 27 July 1917, Barrett shot several snipers when his patrol was forced to withdraw. He covered them as they retired under heavy fire but on reaching his own line safely was killed by a stray shell.

Sergeant John Thomas VC
On 30 November 1917, under enemy fire, Thomas made his way to a building used by the enemy as a listening post. He spent three hours obtaining information on the enemy's preparations, and his actions enabled artillery to break up the German attack.

Captain Arthur Forbes Gordon Kilby VC, MC
During the Battle of Loos, on 25 September 1915, Kilby led his company in an attack on La Basse Canal. Despite losing a foot and sustaining other injuries, he continued to lead his men until he was shot down, urging his men forward until he died.

Lieutenant George Albert Cairns VC
Cairns led his men in an attack on Pagoda Hill on 12 March 1944, continuing to do so after his arm was severed by a Japanese officer, until he collapsed and died of his injuries.

Major Robert Henry Cain VC
Cain led the defence of the Oosterbeek perimeter for several days in September 1944, suffering multiple wounds, but refused rest and medical attention as he continued to lead his men.

Lance-Sergeant John (Jack) Daniel Baskeyfield VC
Baskeyfield commanded two anti-tank guns at Oosterbeck on 20 September 1944, repelling a German attack by destroying

two tanks and a self-propelled gun. Despite being wounded, Baskeyfield refused first aid and continued to use his gun until it was destroyed by enemy fire. He then crawled to another gun and hit another German self-propelled gun before being killed by an enemy tank shell.

The awards received by Cain and Baskeyfield are the only time two Victoria Crosses were received by a single army unit for the same battle.

IN THE AIR

On the night of 31 January 1916, Burton upon Trent and the River Trent were mistaken for Liverpool and the River Mersey by the commander of a German Zeppelin. Fifteen people were killed and seventy-two were injured when the airships dropped bombs on the town. A young man who had remained in Burton as a conscientious objector risked his own life to climb up lampposts and extinguish the streetlights.

RAF Lichfield known locally as Fradley Aerodrome and located 2 miles outside of the city, was used as an operational training station from 1940, preparing crews, many of them Australian, for front-line bombing operations. During the Second World War, it was the busiest airfield in Staffordshire, and was later used to break up aircraft including 900 Typhoons. The first person to touch down on the runway at RAF Lichfield is believed to have been Amy Johnson who had joined the Air Transport Auxiliary, transporting aircraft around the country.

RAF Hednesford was opened in 1938 as the No. 6 School of Technical Training and was used for National Service Training between 1950 and 1956. Afterwards, the site became a resettlement camp for Hungarian refugees. In 1959, the former airfield was sold to Staffordshire County Council and became part of Cannock Chase Country Park.

RAF Wheaton Aston was built in 1941 as a training base for mainly American pilots. After the war, some of the accommodation was used as a Polish resettlement camp.

RAF Hixon was opened in May 1942 and was home to No. 30 OTU (Operation Training Unit), which formed in June of that year and flew Wellington Bombers. The site was closed in November 1962.

RAF Seighford to the north of Stafford opened in January 1943 as a satellite to RAF Hixon and closed in 1947. The site is currently leased by the Staffordshire Gilding Club.

RAF Abbots Bromley acted as a satellite to RAF Burnaston in Derbyshire and comprised of two grass runways and was a Relief Landing Ground opened in 1940. It was used for some time after the war to store ammunition, finally closing in March 1949.

RAF Tatenhill to the west of Burton upon Trent was built as a satellite for the No. 27 OTU at RAF Lichfield, later becoming a satellite for RAF Wheaton Aston. It was originally called RAF Crossplains. Following the Fauld Disaster in November 1944, the site was used by the RAF School of Explosives, and after the Second World War was used to destroy unwanted ammunition before it was dumped. The airfield is still in use as Tatenhill Airfield.

AIRFIELD ACCIDENTS

Vickers Wellington X HF516 of No. 30 OUT crashed into a building site just inside the airfield boundary at Hixon. Although the pilot and three other crew members escaped before the plane burst into flames, Wireless Operator Sgt A.J. Welstead was trapped in the wreckage by his parachute harness. Cyril Fradley, who was in the area delivering bread, ran into the burning aircraft and dragged Sgt Welstead clear. Sadly, the airman succumbed to his injuries the following day. Fradley was badly burned during the rescue attempt and spent five months recovering in hospital, following which he was awarded the British Empire Medal for his bravery.

During a forced landing at Upper Longdon, Armstrong Whitworth Whitley LA927 of No. 42 OTU crashed into a tree killing all four airmen on board.

Vickers Wellington X NC6788 of No. 30 OTU was hit by a practice bomb dropped by another plane. Although the pilot ordered the crew to abandon the aircraft, they failed to hear and were still in the plane when it crashed at Huntingdon, killing four men and injuring another.

When the port engine of Vickers Wellington X JA533 of No. 30 OTU caught fire, the pilot managed to land the plan safely at Seighford, with all nine men aboard managing to escape.

Three of the five men who lost their lives when Vickers Wellington LP346 of No. 27 OTU crashed 4 miles outside of Lichfield were still only teenagers.

On 1 June 1944, Avron Anson N9738 of 3 (Observers) Advanced Flying Unit crashed into Anson EF927 in mid air, shortly after taking off from Halfpenny Green Airfield with the loss of five lives.

After taking off from Castle Donington on a cross-country exercise, Vickers Wellington X LP397 of No. 28 OTU entered a thunderstorm and crashed into a field alongside the church. All six men on board, five of whom were Canadian, were killed. The site was excavated in the 1970s and a memorial was unveiled at the site of the crash on 12 June 2011.

At 11 a.m. on 27 November 1944, seventy people were killed in an explosion at an underground munitions depot beneath RAF Fauld where around 4,000 tons of bombs and ammunition was being stored. The explosion was heard as far away as London and the surrounding landscape was obliterated, including a farm and a nearby reservoir. The site is now known as the Hanbury Crater, and a memorial to the disaster has been erected nearby. The disaster is the largest ever explosion on British soil.

WARTIME MEMORIALS

The Commonwealth War Cemetery on Cannock Chase contains 386 graves; 97 of these are Commonwealth burials from the First World War and 286 are German. There are also three burials from the Second World War here. The site is cared for by the Commonwealth War Graves Commission.

The Cannock Chase German Military Cemetery was dedicated in June 1967 after the governments of Germany and the United Kingdom agreed that the remains of German military personnel and civilians from both world wars would be interred in a single central cemetery. There are almost 5,000 graves on site with 2,143 from the First World War and 2,786 from the Second World War. There are also ninety-five unknown burials. In the Hall of Honour, there is a bronze sculpture of a fallen warrior by Professor Hans Wimmer and a granite monument to the memory of the crews of four airships shot down in the First World War, all of whom are buried here.

The Katyn Memorial on Cannock Chase was erected by the Anglo-Polish Society in 1979 and unveiled by Stefan Staniszewski whose father was murdered in the massacre at Katyn Forest in Poland in 1940, along with thousands of other Polish officers, religious leaders, intellectuals and members of the professional classes. The stone used comes from the Katyn Forest and beneath it is soil from Warsaw and the forest. The sides of the memorial's plinth are inscribed with the names of the three camps which held the victims: Kozielsk, Starobielsk and Ostaszkow.

On the evening of 30 October 1942, Able Seaman Colin Grazier from Two Gates in Tamworth was one of three men who volunteered to search a German U-boat that had been damaged by their ship HMS *Petard*. Grazier searched the sinking submarine, with First Lt Fasson passing any information they could find to 16-year-old canteen assistant Tommy Brown waiting on the conning tower. The ship lurched and both Grazier and Fasson lost their lives. The information they had passed to Brown enabled the codebreakers at Bletchley Park to crack the Enigma code, thus shortening the Second World War by up to a year. A memorial commemorating the bravery of Grazier and the other two men, in front of St Editha's Church in Tamworth, was unveiled on 27 October 2002. Each of the men are represented by an anchor, and an annual service of remembrance takes place on the Sunday nearest to the day they retrieved the codebooks.

The first national memorial in the UK to honour the 130,000 Sikh men who fought during the First World War was unveiled at the National Memorial Arboretum on 1 November 2015. The memorial was funded via the Kickstarter website, where over 200 people pledged money to the WW1 Sikh Memorial Fund.

At Whittington Parish Church, there is an organ paid for by public subscription, as a memorial to sixteen villagers killed in the First World War. The brass plate at the front is inscribed with the name of the fallen and was made from a shell case brought from Mons battlefield. The church registers also record other First World War deaths, with several servicemen from the military hospital at the nearby barracks and one from Brocton Camp at Cannock Chase buried here in late 1918, their deaths possibly related to the Spanish Influenza pandemic of that year.

The anchor in the grounds of Tamworth Castle once stood at Drayton Manor, brought back from the Crimean War by William Peel, Prime Minister Robert Peel's third son.

12

INSTITUTIONS

HOSPITALS

St George's Hospital, originally known as the General Lunatic Asylum, Stafford, opened in 1818 to house 120 pauper lunatics. It was designed by architect Joseph Potter to resemble a Georgian mansion. The hospital closed in 1995 and the building has since suffered from vandalism and arson.

St Matthew's Hospital, also known as Burntwood Asylum, opened in 1864 and was the second county asylum to be built. The building was designed by William Lambie Moffat and it could accommodate up to 1,000 patients. The hospital was largely self-sufficient, with its own bakery, church, laundry, mortuary and farm. In 1867, a cemetery was consecrated and there are a total of 3,103 bodies interred there, although only a few headstones survive. Between 1940 and 1947, St Matthew's was used as an emergency hospital and received 242 men evacuated from the beaches of Dunkirk. In 1948, the hospital was transferred to the National Health Service and was closed in April 1995. The majority of the buildings were demolished when the site was developed into a housing estate although the administration block and the chapel survive.

St Edward's Hospital, also known as Cheddleton County Mental Asylum, was opened in 1899, the third and final county asylum in the county. The building was designed to house 600 patients, with an equal split between the sexes. After the First World

War, many men suffering from shell shock were brought here. In 2002, the hospital was closed and converted into apartments.

Coton Hill Hospital in Stafford was built in the 1850s and was originally an extension to the county asylum to be known as The Institution for the Insane of Staffordshire and the Adjacent Counties. The Tudor-style building had a chapel, cinema, dance hall, gardens and an orchard but, with the exception of the chapel and the lodges, it was demolished in 1976 when the new Stafford District General Hospital was built on the site.

The Fanny Deakin Maternity Home was opened in 1947 in the borough of Newcastle-under-Lyme. Deakin was the first woman to be elected onto Wolstanton Council, initially as a member of the Labour Party, but later re-elected as a communist, earning her the nickname Red Fanny. After only one of her five children survived into adulthood she campaigned for better maternity care and free milk for the under fives. She met Ramsay McDonald at Downing Street in 1931 and persuaded him to allow one pint of milk a day for pregnant women and free milk for children aged 5 and under. During the opening ceremony of the maternity home, Fanny was asked about whether she had faced many obstacles: 'Yes ... and most of the buggers are standing behind me on this platform today!' At her funeral service in 1968, they draped a red flag over her coffin and played 'Keep Right on to the End of the Road', in memory of the hunger marches she had attended. When the maternity home closed, a ward at the City General Hospital was named the Fanny Deakin Memorial Ward.

Biddulph Grange was given to Stoke-on-Trent Council who subsequently sold it to Lancashire County Council, who used it as a children's hospital, originally known as the North Staffordshire Cripples' Hospital, subsequently Biddulph Grange Orthopaedic Hospital. By 1948, children from both Lancashire and Stoke were admitted and in the 1960s the hospital also began to take adults.

Longton Cottage Hospital was built in 1868 on Mount Pleasant and was later moved to Upper Belgrave Road, on land given by the Duke of Sutherland. Today, the hospital provides outpatient clinics.

The **312 Station Hospital** at Shugborough Park was built during the Second World War for use by the United States Army. There were over 1,000 beds, 500 medical officers and nurses, and it specialised as a psychiatric unit. Between 1945 and 1948, the site was used as a war crimes hospital, and it was suggested that the hospital should be used for civilians although these plans failed to come to fruition.

A **military hospital** was built at Brindley Heath on Cannock Chase in 1916 to serve the training camps at Brocton and Rugeley and to house convalescing soldiers returning from the front.

Tamworth Cottage Hospital was built in 1880 with funds provided by the Reverend William MacGregor. When costs for the building of the hospital exceeded the original estimate, trustees went to inform MacGregor who reassured them that he hadn't promised them £300, but had promised them a hospital. The hospital was closed in the 1990s and is now used as sheltered accommodation.

Royal Stoke University Hospital, formerly known as the University Hospital of North Staffordshire, is a teaching and research hospital. Archaeological investigations revealed that a medieval hospital was located at the same site from the thirteenth century until the sixteenth century.

Lichfield's Victoria Hospital, known locally as 'the Vic' opened on Sandford Street in 1899 to provide medical help for the city's poor. There were initially two wards and in 1910, the hospital was extended with a third public ward, two private wards and an operating theatre. In 1933, it moved to new premises at The Friary and a maternity wing was added in 1941. In 2006, the hospital was demolished and replaced by the **Samuel Johnson Community Hospital**.

St Editha's Hospital was the new name given to the Tamworth workhouse, when it was transferred to the NHS in 1948.

Stafford General Infirmary began in a rented house in Foregate Street in 1766 and was one of the oldest hospitals in the country. The hospital was funded by voluntary subscriptions and patients were admitted on the recommendation of donors.

St Michael's in Lichfield is the former Union Workhouse built in a Tudor style in 1840, one of over forty to have been designed by William Bonython Moffatt and George Gilbert Scott, later to become the country's leading Gothic revival architect. The workhouse became St Michael's Hospital in 1948, following the introduction of the National Health Service.

Guy's Almshouses. Thomas Guy paid for the refurbishment of Tamworth's grammar school, which he attended, and built six almshouses for six poor women at Gungate in Tamworth, enlarging the building in 1692 so that it could also accommodate men. In 1695, Guy was elected MP for Tamworth and built a new town hall in 1702. However, when the people of Tamworth failed to re-elect him in 1707, Guy was outraged at the ingratitude, threatening to pull down the building and abolish the almshouses. The burgesses tried to win him back by offering him re-election to the next Parliament in 1710, but the damage had already been done. Although he left the town hall standing, Guy's revenge on the ungrateful people of Tamworth was to deprive them from benefiting from his almshouses. These restrictions are still in place today and there is a stone plaque above the door of Guy's Almshouses for relations and hamleteers. His generosity was instead directed towards Guy's

Hospital in Southwark, which he personally financed and left over £200,000 to in his will.

LAW AND ORDER

In 1944, the first female police officers joined the Staffordshire Constabulary. The initial remit of the six officers was to deal with problems associated with women and children, but since 1976 female officers have performed the same duties as male officers.

Staffordshire Police Force was formed on 1 April 1974 from the Stafford County Police, the Borough of Newcastle-under-Lyme Police, the City of Lichfield Police, the Stoke-on-Trent City Police and the Staffordshire Constabulary.

HM Prison Drake Hall was used as accommodation for female munitions workers during the Second World War. It became a male open prison in the 1960s but since 1974, Drake Hall has been a women's prison.

HMP Featherstone is a Category C male prison constructed on land previously owned by the Ministry of Defence. In the 1980s, it was discovered that prisoners were making forgeries of work by the potter Bernard Leach. In 1991, Brinsford Prison opened on the same site as a Young Offenders' Institute and Remand Centre.

Lichfield Gaol has been located at the rear of the guildhall since 1548. In July 1820, it was reported that all six of the prisoners being held at the gaol had escaped. In 1801, three men accused of uttering (putting forged money into circulation) spent their last night here before being taken to Gallows Wharf for execution – the last execution to take place in the city.

In 1847, the Inspector of Prisons visited the gaol and found that 'the initials and names of many prisoners were cut deep into the wood work'.

Steep Low, to the west of Alstonefield village, is one of the last places where a gibbet was used for execution.

Gnosall's lock-up dates to 1832 and was designed and built by local architect James Trubshaw of Great Haywood in response to the 'rising unemployment, poaching and agricultural riots in the south'. Originally it stood at the junction of High Street, Brookhouse Road and Stafford Street, but in the 1960s, Staffordshire County Council suggested that the building be moved to the County Museum at Shugborough in order that the junction could be widened. Understandably, the Gnosall Women's Institute were keen that the lock-up remain in the village and set about securing a piece of land where it could be re-erected. As if to prove the council's point about the road being a bit narrow, a lorry ran in to it in 1969 but fortunately didn't cause enough damage to prevent it being rebuilt on its current site on Sellman Street in 1971. Other surviving lock-ups in the county can be found at Alton, Stafford and Penkridge.

Stafford Gaol opened in 1793. In 1916, the prison housed prisoners of war from the Easter Rising including Michael Collins and was closed later that year. When the Second World War broke out, the gaol was re-opened and today it is a Category 'C' prison for male adults.

George Smith, known by the morbid nickname of Throttler Smith, was imprisoned in Stafford Gaol for theft on several occasions. When executioner William Calcraft's assistant turned up drunk to assist at the execution of James Owen and George Thomas, Smith was enlisted to help, later being appointed to the position of public executioner for Staffordshire. His final public execution took place at Stafford Gaol in 1866. Throughout his career he carried out thirty-three public executions and one private one when Christopher Edwards was hanged at Stafford for the murder of his wife in August 1872. Smith was succeeded by George Incher.

In 1612, a person named Hollingbury was tried at Lichfield for stealing lead from the church roof of St Michael's.

In March 1888, a 17-year-old miner from Cannock Chase was put on trial for attempting to wreck trains on the Trent Valley line near Lichfield. After being found guilty, he was sentenced to seven years' imprisonment.

Jack Withers was born in Lichfield and was apprenticed to his father, a butcher. He was forced to join the army and was stationed in Ghent where he forced open a church collection box. Having overstuffed his pockets, some of the coins fell to the ground and made a great deal of noise on the marble floor. He was brought before the cardinal to whom he claimed that he was a Protestant who had entered the church in distress and religious uncertainty. He said he had sworn to the Virgin Mary that if she would give him a sign he would convert to Catholicism. According to Withers, the donation box beneath the statue of Mary had sprung open and he had taken this to be the sign he had asked for. The cardinal proclaimed it a miracle. After stealing a silver crucifix and falling under suspicion, he returned to England where he became a highwayman. Jack Withers robbed a postman, stabbed him and filled his disembowelled body with stones so that it would sink below the surface of a nearby pool. The body was discovered and on 16 April 1703, Withers was hanged for his crime.

In January 1844, Sarah Westwood, a Lichfield woman, was hanged for murdering her husband, the last woman to be executed at Stafford Gaol.

In May 1905, an audit of the Lichfield Workhouse's accounts uncovered a series of irregularities regarding payments received for firewood sold to other institutions and houses in the area. When the full extent of the fraud committed by the master of the workhouse, William Williams, was discovered, dismissal from his post was inevitable. However, the Board of Guardians also had to decide whether the loss of job, salary, accommodation, pension entitlement and reputation was punishment enough, or whether the disgraced master should also face prosecution. After much discussion, it was decided that in the interest of the taxpayers, a trial should take place. On Thursday 15 June 1905, William appeared before magistrates charged with embezzling the monies of the Lichfield Poor Law Union and making false entries into certain books with the intent to defraud. Pleading guilty, William told the bench that he had first started to take small amounts of money to meet some of the expenses arising from the illness of his first wife. After that, whenever he had needed money, he had found it easy to help himself to the firewood money. Whilst William acknowledged that he had done wrong, he believed there was no cowardice on his part, having admitted his offences like a man and repaying the amounts he had taken. Whilst the embezzlement charge could be dealt with by the magistrates, the charge of falsifying books was apparently more serious and would have to be dealt with at a higher court. His representative, Mr Jackson of Walsall, appealed to the mercy of the prosecution, describing how his client had 'lost everything in life dear to him' and spoke of 'the suffering and hardship which must inevitably fall on his family' as a result. The magistrates did show mercy and the case for falsifying accounts was withdrawn. In respect of the embezzlement charge, William was ordered to pay £49 12s in fines and costs.

Behind the ostentatious facade of Fisherwick Hall, the Chichester family finances were in jeopardy. The Marquess of Donegall's eldest son, George Augustus, had a gambling problem and was running up debts faster than his father could settle them. In 1794, George found himself in a debtors' gaol. He was released a year later, thanks to moneylender Sir Edward May. This solved the problem of his immediate situation, but left George with an obligation to marry the disreputable May's illegitimate daughter, Anna. Apparently, this was the final straw for Donegall and, though he could do nothing about his troubled heir inheriting his title and much of the family estates, he left whatever he could to his younger son Lord Spencer Stanley Chichester, including the family home at Fisherwick.

In Tamworth in 1337 a man called John le White junior was fined 2d for 'evacuating his bowels to the abomination of neighbours and passers-by'.

Laurence Shirley, 4th Earl Ferrers, was hanged at Tyburn in 1760 for murdering his steward. A new type of gallows was used for his execution but they malfunctioned, failing to kill him, which meant the hangman had to finish him off by pulling on his legs.

John Naden of Leek was condemned to hang at his
master's door and then taken to Gun Heath where
he would hang in chains after confessing to cutting
his employer's throat with his own knife.

Nicholas, son of William of Colton, stabbed
Adam, son of Hereward, in a brawl and took
sanctuary in Colton church.

Juliana Gayton was accused of being involved
in the murder of her husband by his servants
at Stourton Castle in Kinver Forest on 11 April
1316. The decapitated body of Sir Thomas
Murdak was cut into quarters and dumped in the
grounds of his manor of Edgecote. Three days later, Juliana
married Sir John Vaux, keeper of Kinver Forest and Stourton
Castle. In September 1317, Robert Ruggele, a servant of Sir
Thomas, was put on trial and implicated six others including
Vaux and Juliana. After a trial lasting three days in January
1321, Juliana was found guilty of petty treason and ordered to
be burned at the stake, although some sources say the sentence
was later commuted to hanging. Her husband, Vaux, was found
guilty of bigamy but later acquitted of all charges after spending
several years imprisoned in the Tower of London.

In 1965, police were called to the loft of the Nicolson Institute
in Leek to investigate the discovery of a dismembered body
found in a barrel by a workman. The head was missing as were
the limbs, and rumours of murder and foul play were rife. The
following day, the pathologist confirmed that the body was in
fact that of a dissected orangutan although the mystery of how it
came to be in the roof space of the institute remained a mystery.

EDUCATION

The University of Keele

Keele University was established in 1949 as the University College of North Staffordshire. The original accommodation consisted of Second World War army huts and the institution had no books when it first opened. However, thanks to librarian Stanley Stewart, around 200,000 were accumulated within a decade, with a library opening in 1962. The estate had been in the Sneyd family since 1540. The college became a university in 1962, opened by the Queen Mother and Princess Margaret.

On 28 October 1970, a strange protest was carried out by around 300 students. They surrounded the Clock House and attempted to levitate the building up into the air using psychic powers. Some of the protestors claimed that they succeeded in raising the building around six feet off the ground.

Another infamous protest which took place was to declare the existence of a Free Republic of Keele, in response to education cuts in 1980. The Republic issued passports, established border controls, sent a declaration of independence to Margaret Thatcher and also requested that they were recognised by the UN.

Keele Observatory was established in the 1960s when a telescope was acquired from the observatory at Oxford University. It's first director was Dr Ron Maddison and it was built on the site of a pavilion built by former owners of Keele Hall in the seventeenth century. If you travel east from Observatory Hill, you will not find higher ground until reaching the Ural Mountains in Russia.

Schools

A plaque on the old schoolmaster's house at Hopwas reads: 'This house was built at the charge of Mr Thomas Barnes native of this place and a citizen of London in the year of our Lord

1717 for the dwelling of a person to teach the children of this village to read English.' It's a great example of the local lad-made-good story, as Thomas Barnes was abandoned as a baby, and discovered in a barn by villagers who gave him a surname to represent his humble beginnings as well as providing him with an education, before he became a successful merchant in the capital.

In around 1813, Cowperthwaite Smith was appointed headmaster of Lichfield Grammar School with a salary of £170 per annum, plus rent-free accommodation. At the time, board, lodging and tuition was being charged at between 40 and 50 guineas a year for each scholar. In 1828, according to the Account of Public Charities in England and Wales, there were eighteen boarders, and around thirty to forty students in total. It goes on to say that the only scholars receiving their education free at the school were the 'six children of poor men born within the City' (who were also given money for books, and slightly more curiously brooms, when the school was first endowed). The people of Lichfield were apparently not happy that their grammar school was no longer a free school. By the

end of Cowperthwaite Smith's time as headmaster in the 1840s, no boys at all were coming to the school. Allegations were made in the *Wolverhampton Chronicle* that Lichfield Grammar School had been closed for six years due to the misconduct of the master. It claimed he was violent towards the children in his care, and that 'his treatment of two boys on two separate occasions subjected his modes of punishment to investigation before the magistrates [,] one boy having subsequently confined to his bed under surgical advice for a fortnight'.

MUSEUMS

The Hayward Puppet Collection is now at the Staffordshire County Museum but was originally the Marionette Theatre and Puppet Museum created at Abbots Bromley in 1975 by touring puppeteer Douglas Hayward.

The Airspace Gallery is an artist-led project in Stoke-on-Trent, opened in May 2006 by Turner Prize-winner Martin Creed with a focus on contemporary art and providing studio space and development opportunities to a broad range of artists.

The Ancient High House, Stafford, built in 1594, is the largest timber-framed town house in England and is now a museum, each room decorated to reflect a different era in the building's history.

Erasmus Darwin House in Lichfield is a museum dedicated to the eighteenth-century poet and physician and founding member of the Lunar Society, who lived here from 1758 to 1781.

Lichfield Museum, located in St Mary's Church in the Market Square, was opened by the Earl of Lichfield in May 1981 and features a heritage exhibition telling the city's history while the Muniment Room holds the ancient city charters. The museum also houses the Staffordshire Millenium Embroideries, created by Sylvia Everitt, which tell the story of Staffordshire through a series of panels, one for each century of the last millennium. Visitors to the museum are also able to climb the church spire for panoramic views across the city and surrounding area.

The Museum of Cannock Chase occupies the site of the former Valley Colliery, a training pit for those starting work in the local coal industry and tells the story of the area's industrial heritage.

Robert Greene's Museum was at his home on Sadler Street, Lichfield. Sadler is now Market Street and the house has long since vanished; the only trace is a plaque attached to a wall. Highlights from the collection include 'the Earthen Vessel found (with several others of smaller size) in the Walls of the late Conventual Church of Fairwell near Lichfield, at the time it was taken down in order to be rebuilt' and also, 'Part of the Porch, under which stood Lord Brooke General of the Parliament forces, when he receiv'd a mortal wound in his forehead, by some shot from the Battlements of the great Steeple of the Cathedral Church of Lichfield, the force of which was abated by the bullets passing through the above piece of Board', a 'small Leaden box, in which is contained some Relicks, and Silver Lace, found in an ancient Leaden Coffin in the Cathedral Church of Lichfield 1748', as well as the Horn of the Sea Unicorn, 5ft and 6in long, the head of a pike weighing 40lbs, taken at Burton upon Trent and balls of hair found in the stomach of a cow. After Greene died in 1793, the collection was sold by his son to various collectors. Some of it was bought back to Lichfield by his grandson, Richard Wright, and displayed in a new museum in the Cathedral Close, which then moved to a property in the north of Dam Street. When Wright died in 1821, the collection was broken up again, although some items did remain in the city.

The Marquess of Donegal spent a small fortune acquiring an eclectic collection of antiquities and other objects for a private museum at his home Fisherwick Hall. A letter written in 1788 reports that Donegall 'expended £20,000 on books not yet open and £10,000 on shells not yet unpacked'. According to a list drawn up by the Reverend Stebbing Shaw, amongst the many curiosities in the private museum were 'cases & drawers full of shells, fossils, stones, roman coins and medals', 'indian dresses and old books', 'a miniature of Mary, Queen of Scots, painted from life for a gold locket' and 'a brass figure of Antioch with a Greek inscription around his hat'. The whereabouts of many of these objects is unknown, but we do know that one extraordinary item from the collection – a virginal previously owned by the Virgin Queen herself – is now kept at the Victoria & Albert Museum.

13

MUSIC, LITERATURE AND TELEVISION

Dr Samuel Johnson, born in Lichfield in 1709, was one of the most important literary figures of the eighteenth century and, according to the *Oxford English Dictionary of Quotations*, is the second most-quoted Englishman of all time. Despite the success of his *Dictionary of the English Language*, completed in 1755 and earning him the nickname 'Dictionary Johnson', he struggled financially until he was awarded a pension by the king in 1762. In 1759, he wrote *The History of Rasselas, Prince of Abissinia* in just one week in order to help pay his mother's funeral expenses. Johnson died on 13 December 1784 and is buried in Poets' Corner, Westminster Abbey, alongside several of those he had written about in his last great work, *The Lives of the English Poets*. In 1999, the Samuel Johnson Prize for Non-Fiction was founded, but was renamed The Baillie Gifford Prize in 2015 after its new sponsors.

Britain's first female poet laureate Carol Ann Duffy grew up in Stafford and attended Stafford Girls' High School. Stafford makes an appearance in many of her poems including 'The Laughter of Stafford Girls' High' and 'Stafford Afternoons'.

Sir Gawain and the Green Knight is one of the best known of the King Arthur stories, written by an anonymous poet in the fourteenth century. J.R.R. Tolkien translated the poem and identified the language as being that of the north Midlands. Many of the locations mentioned in the work are believed to be places in Staffordshire, including Lud's Church, which has been identified as the site of the Green Chapel.

Philip Larkin was sent from his first term at Oxford to stay with his Uncle Alfred in Lichfield, as his parents thought their Coventry home to be too dangerous, following the November 1940 air raid on the town. It may have been safe but Larkin's early opinion of Lichfield was, 'God, this place is dull', and later wrote, 'Makes you appreciate Oxford you know, coming to a lonely spot like this'. Larkin wrote three poems in Lichfield, 'Christmas 1940', 'Ghosts' and 'Out in the Lane', although only the latter made it into his *Collected Poems*. Larkin's mother and father are buried in the churchyard of St Michael's, along with many other members of the family. On one visit to the family graves, Larkin discovered the headstone of his namesake who died in December 1879, and afterwards wrote to his friend, 'I reeled away conscious of a desire to vomit into a homburg hat'.

Izaak Walton is best known as author of the *Compleat Angler*, published in 1653 and said to be the second most reprinted book in English, after the King James Bible. Walton did not only write about his favourite pastime, about which he said, 'God never did make a more calm, quiet, innocent recreation than angling', he was also a biographer of notable clergymen and theologians. In contrast to his tranquil hobby, during the Civil War, Royalist supporter Walton risked his life to deliver the Lesser George, a gold and diamond jewel, which had been hidden in a Staffordshire farmhouse, to a prisoner in the Tower of London who subsequently escaped and delivered it to the exiled King Charles II. On his death he left his half-timbered cottage at Shallowford to his hometown of Stafford. The cottage on the banks of the River Dove was purchased by the Izaak Walton Trust in 1923 and is now a museum.

In the summer of 1806, Jane Austen visited her cousin Edward Cooper, rector of St Michael's and All Angels in Hamstall

Ridware. However, Jane's reluctance is revealed in a letter she wrote which said, 'Edward Cooper is so kind as to want us all to come to Hamstall this Summer, instead of going to the sea, but we are not so kind as to mean to do it. The summer after, if you please Mr Cooper, but for the present we greatly prefer the sea to all our relations'. It is believed the village near Rugeley may have provided the inspiration for the fictional 'Delaford' in *Sense and Sensibility*.

Anna Seward, known as the Swan of Lichfield after publishing her *Elegy on Captain Cook*, lived at the Bishop's Palace in the Close with her father, after he was appointed the canon residentiary at Lichfield Cathedral. Seward was an active member of Lichfield's literary community, encouraged by Erasmus Darwin, whose biography she would go on to write after his death. After her death on 25 March 1809, her poetic works were edited and published by Sir Walter Scott.

When Jonathan Swift, author of *Gulliver's Travels*, stayed at the Four Crosses Inn near Cannock, en route to Ireland, he scratched a verse insulting the landlord's wife into one of the window panes. Although the exact wording has been lost along with the pane of glass, it is thought to have said something along the following lines: 'Fool to put up four crosses at your door! Put up your wife, as she's crosser than all four!'

Anne Wilmot-Horton of Croxall Hall prompted Lord Byron to write his famous poem beginning with the lines 'She walks in beauty, like the night' after they met at a ball in London.

Elizabeth Gaskell, author of *Cranford* and *North and South*, was a close friend of Caroline Davenport who married Lord Hatherton of Teddesley Hall, Penkridge, in 1852. When visiting Caroline, Gaskell met Mr Burton, the head gardener at Teddesley and published the story of how he had been the gardener to the Shah of Persia in *Household Words*, a magazine run by Charles

Dickens. As Lady Hatherton, Caroline persuaded her husband to open the gardens of Teddesley Hall to the public, to launch a scheme of medical insurance in Penkridge, and in 1853 signed the anti-slavery petition of British Women 'An Affectionate and Christian Address of Many Thousands of Women of Great Britain and Ireland to their Sisters, the Women of the USA', which was presented to Harriet Beecher Stowe, the author of *Uncle Tom's Cabin*. On Stowe's visit to England she was shown around London by Lady Hatherton.

Born in Hanley in May 1867, Arnold Bennett based his novels in five of the six towns that make up Stoke-on-Trent: Tunstall, Burslem, Hanley, Stoke and Longton became Turnhill, Bursley, Hanbridge, Knype and Longshaw. Fenton was excluded and Bennett explained this was because the 'I' in five sounded more striking that the 'I' in six, and that he'd chosen to include Tunstall rather than the larger Fenton as the former had a more distinct identity.

In 1916, J.R.R. Tolkein was stationed at one of the First World War training camps on Cannock Chase, and his new wife Edith moved to a cottage at the nearby village of Great Haywood to be near him. Tolkien was sent to the Western Front but returned home after contracting trench fever and spent the winter with Edith at Great Haywood. During this time, Tolkien began to write the *Book of Lost Tales*. The village of Tavrobel in 'The Tale of the Sun and the Moon' has been identified as being based on Great Haywood according to Tolkien's son Christopher, and the bridge where the two rivers, the Gruir and the Afros, meet is thought to have been inspired by the Essex Bridge across where the Trent and the Sow merge, with nearby Shugborough Hall possibly reimagined as the House of a Hundred Chimneys.

Hayslope, the fictional village where George Eliot set her first novel *Adam Bede*, is based on Ellastone, where her grandfather lived and where her father spent his early years working as a carpenter.

Thomas Day is best known for *The History of Sandford and Merton*, one of the earliest novels written for children. Day arrived in Lichfield in 1770 with one of the two young women he had 'adopted' from an orphanage with a view to shaping one of them into being a perfect wife. Day had already discarded one of the girls, Lucretia, and rented out Stowe House where he attempted to train the other, Sabrina, through a series of experiments. As well as dripping hot wax on her arms and firing pistols at her petticoats in a bid to improve her stoicism, Day also forced Sabrina into the cold waters of nearby Stowe Pool despite her inability to swim. As she approached the age of 14, Day abandoned his hopes of creating a perfect wife and sent Sabrina to a boarding school in Sutton Coldfield. The story of Day's experiment is believed to have inspired George Bernard Shaw's 1913 play *Pygmalion*.

Vera Brittain was born in Newcastle-under-Lyme and her best-selling memoir *The Testament of Youth* is based on her experience of the First World War, in which she served as a nurse. Her daughter, the politician Shirley Williams, planted a copper beech in Brampton Park near to where she was born. A sculpture of a woman sitting on a bench, reading a letter of sympathy after losing a loved one in the war, was inspired by Brittain's work and a quote from the book is at the figure's feet. Vera herself lost her fiancé, her brother and two friends in the conflict. Vera died in March 1970 and her ashes were scattered on the grave of her brother Edward in the Granezza British Cemetery in Italy.

A.N. Wilson, born in Stone, began training to be a priest and had a teaching career before concentrating on writing. Wilson is a journalist and author of novels, popular histories and biographies, including books on Leo Tolstoy, Jesus Christ and Irish Murdoch.

Staffordshire's first poet laureate was Mal Dewhirst from Tamworth, who was appointed in October 2012.

Rhoda Broughton was brought up in an Elizabethan manor house in Broughton, and would later use the family home as a setting for her novels, some of which were considered risqué. Anthony Trollope commented in his autobiography that 'she has made her ladies do and say things which ladies would not do and say'. Although Rhoda was known as the 'Queen of the Circulating Libraries', her novels were banned by them until the 1870s. Despite her critics, her work was popular to the extent that the captain of HMS *Alert* named a mountain 'Mount Rhoda' to commemorate the fact that he and his crew had enjoyed reading her books during their time at sea.

Ralph Griffiths started out in business as a watchmaker in Stone, before moving to London to work as a bookseller and launching the *Monthly Review*. In 1750, with his brother Fenton, he published John Cleland's *Fanny Hill*, one of history's most banned books, in two instalments, causing the brothers to be arrested and charged with 'corrupting the King's subjects'. It seems however that the king's subjects were happy to be corrupted, as profits from the book earned Griffiths a reputed £10,000.

The Quaker writer Mary Howitt, author of the poem 'The Spider and the Fly', lived in Uttoxeter for much of her life. Some of her poems and novels were influenced by the town, which also inspired her love of natural history, as also featured in her books. Three of her poems were recently displayed in the town's bus shelters by the Uttoxeter Arts Festival Committee and the town's Howitt Crescent is named after her.

In 1864, a young couple called Mr and Mrs Lockwood visited Rudyard Lake and fell in love with the place. A year later, their son was born in India and they named him after the lake in Staffordshire.

The *Wench is Dead*, a novel in the Inspector Morse series, was based on the murder of Christina Collins in 1839 after Colin

Dexter was introduced to the story by a local historian and former head teacher from Rugeley. Dexter spent 'a good many fruitful hours' at the William Salt Library in Stafford consulting contemporary newspaper reports. The book won the British Crime Writers' Association Gold Dagger Award for best crime novel of the year in 1989, and it was later filmed as an episode in the Inspector Morse series.

Hanley appears in Charles Dickens' *Hard Times* as 'Coke Town', as Bernard Shaw explains in the introduction to the book in 1912: 'Coketown, which you can see for yourself in all its grime in the Potteries (the real name of it is Hanley in Staffordshire on the London and North Western Railway).' Dickens once found himself in Stafford for the night, in between trains and described the town, "as dull and dead [a]town as anyone could not desire to see".' He christened The Swan Hotel, where he stayed, 'The Dodo in the High Street', and described it as having seen better days, complaining about its tired furnishings and the empty larder.

MUSIC AND TELEVISION

Gertie Gitana was really Gertie Astbury from Longport. A street in Hanley now bears the name of the music hall star who first appeared on stage at the age of 4 under the name Little Gitana. The Stage Door pub, once named after her, still has her portrait above the door.

The official Elvis Presley Fan Club of Great Britain, first founded in 1957, is based in Cheadle and has over 20,000 members from all over the world.

Singer and former member of Take That, Robbie Williams was born in Stoke-on-Trent and set up a charity called Give it Sum, aimed at improving local conditions and strengthening community life in his home town. Robbie is also the patron of the Donna Louise Trust offering respite care to children with life limiting illnesses. Williams is also a life-long supported of Port Vale and in February 2006 became the majority shareholder at the club, although the club went into administration in March 2012, and his share and most of his investment was lost.

Yvonne Burgess, born in Newcastle-under-Lyme in 1940 and known as 'the Vera Lynn of the Potteries', adopted the stage name Jackie Trent, inspired by the river. Jackie reached number one with the song 'Where are you now' with co-writer, and later husband, Tony Hatch, knocking The Beatles' 'Ticket to Ride' off the top spot. Together the couple wrote more than 400 songs for artists including Val Doonican, Dean Martin and Petula Clark. In 1984, the couple were asked to write a theme tune for a proposed TV show provisionally titled *Ramsay Street* and came up with a song based on the idea of good neighbours, which was written and recorded in one day. The song was so popular with the show's producers that they changed the name of the series to *Neighbours*. The couple also wrote the Stoke City anthem 'We'll be with you', released under the name The Potters, for the 1972 League Cup Final. The song is still played at Stoke City home games.

Calwich Abbey was visited regularly by George Frideric Handel, said to have worked on both *Messiah* and his *Water Music* during his time there.

Thor's Cave was the location for the video to The Verve's 1993 single 'Blue' and was also pictured on the cover of the band's first album, *A Storm in Heaven*.

Ian Fraser Kilmister better known as Lemmy was born on Christmas Eve 1945 in Burslem, Stoke-on-Trent. He worked as Jimi Hendrix's roadie and played in several bands before forming Motorhead in 1975. As singer and bassist he was the only consistent member in the band best known for their single 'Ace of Spades' released in 1980.

Saul 'Slash' Hudson was raised by his father and grandparents in Stoke-on-Trent but moved to Los Angeles when he was 5. His second live album entitled *Made in Stoke 24/7/11* was recorded at Victoria Hall on 24 July 2011.

Hamstall Ridware is the name of one of the two members of UK-based downtempo band Sundae Club.
The 1972 Labi Siffre album *Crying Laughing Loving Lying* features a track entitled 'Cannock Chase'.

Green Day named the first song on their *Insomniac* album 'Armatage Shanks' [*sic*] after seeing the name of the bathroom fixtures manufacturer on a visit to England.

One version of the folk ballad 'Bold William Taylor' begins:

> I'll sing you a song about two lovers,
> Who from Lichfield town they came,
> The young man's name was William Taylor,
> The lady's name was Sarah Gray …

The song goes on to tell the tale of William, who leaves Lichfield to go and fight a war, and Sarah who decides she too will become a soldier in order to be reunited with her true love. She disguises herself as a sailor but after she suffers a wardrobe malfunction aboard the ship she is working on, it becomes apparent to the captain of the ship that she is in fact a woman. Understandably curious, the captain wants to know what she's doing on board his ship and Sarah explains that she's there looking for her lover. The captain gives her the devastating news that William Taylor has gone off and married a rich young lady but tells her that if she rises before the break of day she'll find him out walking with his new wife. Sarah does just that and, on spying the happy couple together, calls for a sword and pistol and shoots William dead. In this version, the captain is so impressed he puts Sarah in command of the ship and all his men. All's fair in love and war as they say.

TELEVISION

Comedian, author and television presenter Dave Gorman was born in Stafford in 1971 and was awarded an honorary doctorate from Staffordshire University in 2006.

Actress Helen Baxendale grew up in Shenstone and went to school in Lichfield where the British sitcom *Cuckoo*, in which she stars, is set.

In 2006, the BBC programme *Top Gear* held a challenge at Rudyard Lake to see which of the three presenters had created the best amphibious car.

Ken Barrie, born in Tunstall, Stoke-on-Trent, provided the original voice for *Postman Pat*, also singing the theme tune which spent fifteen weeks in the top 75.

Barnes Hall at Keele University is named after Sir George Barnes, a pioneer in British broadcasting, who was the first controller of the BBC *Third Programme* (now Radio 3) and later the director of BBC Television. He retired from the BBC in 1956 to become the third Principal of the University College of North Staffordshire, as Keele was then known.

Film director and screenwriter Shane Meadows was born and grew up in Uttoxeter and won the British Independent Film Award for Best British Independent Film in 2006 and a BAFTA for *This is England*. Sequels to the film were adapted into television serials, ending with *This Is England '90*, screened in 2015.

Comedian and chat show host Alan Carr donated prize money of almost £90,000, won on TV quiz show *The Million Pound Drop*, to the British Wildlife Rescue Centre at Amerton Farm near Stafford.

The 100th edition of the TV show *Tiswas* was broadcast from Hednesford Hills Raceway in the 1970s.

In 2015, the Gladstone Pottery Museum featured in the BBC series *24 Hours in the Past*, where six celebrities experienced a range of occupations from the Victorian era.

ABOUT THE AUTHOR

KATE GOMEZ lives in Lichfield and is currently studying Linguistics at the University of Wolverhampton. She works in community development and writes the popular local history blog, lichfieldlore.co.uk and also runs the social history group Lichfield Discovered, which offers a variety of walks and visits to places of interest in and around Staffordshire. Kate is involved in a number of community history projects, including work to save the Grade II* Listed Sandfields Pumping Station in Lichfield for the community and to promote the heritage and history of Woodhouse Community Farm, which once formed part of the Fisherwick estate.